1500 WAYS
to
ESCAPE
the
HUMAN JUNGLE

by Vernon Howard

Published by

NEW LIFE FOUNDATION
PO BOX 2230
PINE, ARIZONA 85544
(520) 476-3224
www.anewlife.org

ISBN 0-911203-01-X

ABOUT
VERNON HOWARD

Vernon Howard broke through to another world. He saw through the illusion of suffering and fear and loneliness. From 1965 until his death in 1992 he wrote books and conducted classes which reflect a degree of skill and understanding that may be unsurpassed in modern history. Tape recordings of many of his class talks are available.

Today more than 8 million readers worldwide enjoy his exceptionally clear and inspiring presentations of the great truths of the ages. His books are widely used by doctors, psychiatrists, psychologists, counselors, clergymen, educators and people from all walks of life. All his teachings center around the one grand theme: *"There is a way out of the human problem and anyone can find it."*

Vernon Howard Books and Booklets

There is a Way Out
Psycho-Pictography
A Treasury of Trueness
The Power of Esoterics
Pathways to Perfect Living
Treasury of Positive Answers
Mystic Path to Cosmic Power
50 Ways to See Thru People
Be Safe in a Dangerous World
Your Power of Natural Knowing
50 Ways to Get Help from God
700 Inspiring Guides to a New Life
Women—50 Ways to See Thru Men
Conquer Anxiety and Frustration
Practical Exercises for Inner Harmony

And Many Others

CONTENTS

LET THIS BOOK GUIDE YOUR LIFE

Every great idea can be stated in a single sentence–and should be! One clear and true sentence can be worth more than a library of books. You now hold in your hands the simplified secret wisdoms of the ages. Here are four ways to use this book for rich results:

1. Read with a relaxed and yet alert mind, connecting these truths with your own needs and questions. Write down the numbers of those offering special help, and review them often. You may wish to memorize your favorites.

2. See the practical accuracy of these teachings; for example, notice how precisely they describe human nature. Realize that the presented solutions are equally accurate. Test them freely in daily affairs. Let them work for you, which they are eager to do.

3. Use the *Reading Programs* on the next page. Read the listed sentences, absorbing their messages deeply.

4. Join or form a study group for discussing these higher principles. You may write the New Life Foundation for aid in locating a local class.

We must get to the point in our lives. What is the point? To become a new kind of man or woman, having inner command and outer excellence. We can live with mental independence of the human jungle, even while active in it. This book guides you toward the kind of life you have always wanted, so release its powers into your day and enjoy your new life.

Vernon Howard

Reading Programs

For Pleasant Feelings: 150, 248, 305, 499, 503, 530, 674, 752, 877, 912, 1058, 1094, 1330, 1375, 1436, 1490.

For Enriching Actions: 168, 217, 252, 267, 355, 417, 485, 603, 679, 717, 901, 940, 1035, 1181, 1297, 1327.

For Curious Facts: 16, 27, 83, 113, 148, 290, 490, 627, 688, 742, 818, 862, 945, 1110, 1222, 1326.

For Handling People: 11, 75, 180, 279, 312, 522, 556, 665, 801, 875, 1021, 1063, 1117, 1189, 1257, 1371.

For Reliable Guides: 223, 405, 425, 461, 561, 653, 718, 786, 896, 958, 995, 1007, 1060, 1236, 1353, 1421.

For Living Lightly: 119, 179, 212, 368, 407, 661, 776, 894, 932, 974, 1012, 1061, 1241, 1361, 1405, 1487.

For Secret Powers: 101, 186, 466, 641, 707, 761, 800, 905, 939, 1025, 1048, 1165, 1232, 1311, 1417, 1475.

For Solving Problems: 103, 201, 361, 423, 590, 657, 683, 768, 881, 961, 985, 1093,

1105, 1250, 1279, 1385.

For Commanding Life: 162, 218, 390, 454, 585, 748, 771, 828, 921, 980, 1017, 1077, 1127, 1266, 1422, 1495.

For Cheery News: 145, 199, 240, 455, 486, 523, 600, 726, 969, 1034, 1095, 1270, 1344, 1395, 1441, 1480.

For Avoiding Troubles: 5, 140, 291, 396, 508, 526, 575, 778, 866, 882, 968, 993, 1006, 1066, 1263, 1406.

For New Strength: 198, 298, 350, 402, 538, 607, 712, 917, 1004, 1038, 1052, 1101, 1138, 1300, 1380, 1464.

For Banishing Confusions: 32, 124, 176, 259, 482, 531, 614, 690, 715, 753, 836, 910, 935, 1023, 1333, 1438.

For Healing Secrets: 134, 229, 310, 406, 511, 630, 709, 767, 911, 972, 1019, 1089, 1132, 1206, 1321, 1478.

For Saving Energy: 215, 318, 453, 672, 728, 799, 839, 902, 964, 1010, 1207, 1244, 1340, 1384, 1423, 1470.

For True Rewards: 85, 197, 206, 400, 434, 507, 660, 725, 796, 946, 990, 1028, 1075,

1193, 1305, 1489.

For Ending Anxiety: 192, 221, 262, 358, 420, 534, 579, 652, 737, 889, 922, 1002, 1121, 1285, 1317, 1412.

For Healthy Attitudes: 61, 73, 191, 227, 484, 605, 639, 743, 923, 986, 1067, 1082, 1115, 1153, 1341, 1416.

For Finding Yourself: 102, 195, 247, 271, 337, 389, 465, 525, 651, 704, 952, 1001, 1054, 1387, 1432, 1483.

For Swift Progress: 126, 261, 411, 447, 573, 605, 719, 900, 941, 1014, 1045, 1143, 1200, 1266, 1351, 1496.

For Brighter Conditions: 89, 153, 243, 324, 421, 479, 621, 654, 760, 899, 963, 1020, 1041, 1159, 1369, 1485.

For Relieving Tension: 270, 375, 481, 666, 693, 721, 766, 901, 981, 1015, 1040, 1070, 1107, 1287, 1360, 1460.

For Profound Ideas: 24, 186, 204, 317, 354, 597, 637, 734, 781, 810, 944, 973, 1008, 1135, 1231, 1428.

For Inspiring Truths: 139, 196, 297, 384, 429, 474, 496, 581, 681, 703, 784, 948, 1000, 1373, 1401, 1444.

1

Strange Facts About
the Human Jungle

An explorer was lost in the jungles of South America. He struck out in a dozen different directions, but none of them led anywhere. He finally studied a narrow canyon which at first glance had appeared valueless. But his exploration proved that it was the road leading back to camp.

You can have a similar experience. If baffled by life, simply remember that the answer exists in a totally new direction. The purpose of Chapter 1 is to start you off in the direction leading to the truly worthwhile. Your first one hundred steps will acquaint you with the human jungle as it exists in fact. Have no concern if these descriptions of human life seem surprising or shocking or different from your present views. *The right road always seems surprising at first.* But this very surprise is also your first invitation to a much loftier level of living.

Choose freedom. Choose freedom from the human jungle. That is all you need to do in order to start. Your very choice is an expression of affection for the true and the happy. Say with Henry David Thoreau, "I know of no more encouraging fact than the unquestionable ability of a man to elevate his life by a conscious endeavor."

Now step forward with a conscious endeavor to understand human life in order to change *your* life.

Strange Facts About
the Human Jungle

1. Human society is simply men and women pretending that the game of pretense is not going on.

2. Humanity appreciates truth about as much as a squirrel appreciates silver.

3. If you think that his or her happy face is a mask covering unhappiness, you are right.

4. What most men call their conscience is imaginary virtue switching left or right according to self-interest.

5. Observe a man's behavior when told unpleasant truths about himself and you will really know the man.

6. Man has a perfect device for maintaining his darkness, and that device is to say that darkness is light.

7. When someone says he wants to help you, try to see where he wants to help himself.

8. If a man does not understand what it means to be under psychic hypnosis, he is under it.

9. See once and for all that human affairs can improve only when minds awaken from psychic hypnosis.

10. The good performed by awakened individuals is never seen nor appreciated by hypnotized humanity.

11. Your friends will be as careless with your life as they are with their own.

12. Few people realize that other people see them in a totally different way than they see themselves.

13. Calling the wrong the right cannot make a man feel right, and how strange that he never notices this.

14. When someone insists he knows the truth about life, ask him why he needs to nervously insist.

15. Humanity rejects truth, like a hungry man who refuses bread because his dizzy mind thinks it is wood.

16. People wish kindness, yet are incredibly unkind toward themselves by their rejection of truth.

17. When surface personality talks about spiritual matters it distorts everything, never knowing what it is doing against itself and against others.

18. Argument is a valuable evasion of truth to

those who prefer religion to truth.

19. When someone lacks the intelligence to try to understand he covers it up by criticizing.

20. No one is nice unless he can be so without nice possessions and nice advantages.

What Millions Miss

21. Unawakened men by the millions pass an awakened man on the street and never know what they have passed by.

22. Artificiality can be detected by the way its smiles turn to scowls when it is questioned.

23. By wrongly believing that something is necessary and vital we miss the truly necessary and vital.

24. The truly necessary and vital is to realize that we are here on earth to rise above ourselves.

25. The greater a man's distance from rightness the closer he will claim to be.

26. It is a great mistake to believe that the evil get away with it, for they are their own punishment.

27. People say they wish to do heaven's will,

and how curious that it is the same thing *they* want to do.

28. Strangely, man loves his mental fog more then he loves the effort which could dissolve it.

29. It is a healthy shock to deeply see how few people really want to change inwardly.

30. Imaginary life has great power to control and wreck people because it insists it is not imaginary life.

31. One person who blocks his escape is the person who believes he has already escaped.

32. The simplest of facts are unseen by man, for instance, believing that we understand and actual understanding are as different as night and noon.

33. An angel can never be deceived by a demon, but a demon is constantly deceived by other demons.

34. A demon consists of a negative thought, a cherished delusion, a clever falsehood, a destructive emotion.

35. The worst decision in life is to choose egotism over the opportunity to wake up.

36. Society will always deceive you when you ask it, "What is life all about?"

37. A million people can declare that wrong is right, but all will suffer from the wrongness.

38. Man leans on his frail opinions and then wonders why he always feels about to fall.

39. Conflict and despair dwell in a man to the precise degree that he cannot be told what he is really like.

40. Everyone who foolishly marches in step with the mechanical masses proudly believes he is independent.

The Basic Human Mistake

41. The basic human mistake can be explained by saying that men and women live from imaginary identities instead of from their real natures.

42. The cruel taskmaster is nothing more than a man's own psychic ignorance which he covers by calling it wisdom.

43. Immature man is like a frightened child, alone in a darkening room, not seeing the nearby light switch.

44. Notice how individuals and organizations do the opposite of their promise, and you will begin to understand human nature.

45. When weak people pretend to be strong they do the one thing that prevents attainment of real strength.

46. Having strong personal beliefs derived from social conditioning is not at all the same as having a clear conscience derived from cosmic consciousness.

47. When told that men live in delusion, everyone thinks he is the exception, which is part of his delusion.

48. It is a waste of time to preach to a bat about the glories of sunshine.

49. One of man's most amazing self-deceptions is his pretense of having self-control while his life flies apart before his very eyes.

50. A successful day for many people is one in which no one discovered what he is really thinking.

51. A true teaching explains what life is all about, while a false teaching hides what it is all about.

52. Can you think of anything more ridiculous than praising and paying people who lead you astray?

53. Remember, the human jungle is thick with

deceptive signs which describe it as a nice and sincere place.

54. A man's failure to question the ideas by which he lives keeps his life as it is.

55. No one can demand to live according to his fantasies and then demand that someone else pay for their unhappy consequences.

56. One man is the echo of the next man, both wrongly assuming they are original sources.

57. Truth replies only when first hearing sincere questions, and how few it hears.

58. The reason people are frustrated is simply because a lie cannot be turned into a truth.

59. A confused mind calls itself a clear mind, and that explains the entire human horror story.

60. Those who pretend to know the truth have no choice but to try to deceive and injure you.

A Courageous Statement

61. These teachings are for those who state, "I have played the self-deceiving game long enough and am tired of it."

62. A type of sheeplike conformity rarely realized by people is the conformity of being deluded.

63. When society praises loyalty it is simply pledging allegiance to its own neurosis.

64. The more contradictions in a man the more he likes to accuse others of having contradictions.

65. The refusal of rescue can take many forms, as with the preference for bitterness over insight.

66. What vanity calls personal choice is simply the attraction or repulsion of exterior things.

67. A chief feature of false life is that it cannot stand alone, but frantically demands allies to support its false positions.

68. A real conscience is as high above society's moralities as a star is above a sheep.

69. Nothing in the world is what it seems because the viewer himself is not what he seems.

70. A person immersed in psychic sleep will always deny it, for his very sleep prevents him from hearing about and understanding his actual condition.

71. People who make the human jungle the horror that it is often pose as experts in escaping it.

72. Truth can be explained with simple words, but deluded man thinks that the obscure is the profound.

73. A simple admission that one's life does not make sense as now lived could be the great turning point.

74. What do you expect from a world that glorifies weakness by calling it strength?

75. A weak person's duty is to try to shove his responsibilities onto you, and your duty is to refuse them.

76. A man's wish to exploit other people is his unconscious invitation to other people to exploit him in return.

77. Demons disguised as angels will always claim that angels are demons disguised as angels.

78. Self-deception is so subtle that perhaps one person in a million really understands its danger.

79. The great test of sincerity is whether we are willing to hear about and examine self-deception.

80. A false path must be tensely and angrily defended by those it has deceived.

The Banquet is Ready
81. The banquet is always on the table, but

hungry men and women refuse to approach.

82. A man lacking courage to make his own decisions will have plenty of nerve to criticize the decisions of others.

83. Can a person who remains in secret internal confusion ever do what is truly right for himself?

84. If your friends want to angrily fight life, you can only let them do so, while you live above life.

85. Confused humanity mistakes mere movement for progress, but real progress must include an awakening of inner essence.

86. Remember, destructive egotism never calls itself egotism, but masquerades as love, generosity, helpfulness.

87. If heaven existed as a physical building on earth, human beings would remodel it to make it right.

88. One of society's absurd delusions is that the spending of money can cure something.

89. It is possible to have ideas of cosmic quality, and they alone can do good to the world.

90. Anyone lacking the ability to listen cannot listen when told of his inability to listen.

91. One cunning trick of false light is to solemnly warn you against false light.

92. Cosmic sunshine exists to those who have learned to drop their strange love for shadows.

93. Trying to change conditions without changing ourselves is as impossible as dry water.

94. A chief feature of an unawakened human being is his lack of interest in anything above his own neurosis.

95. The healing facts can penetrate a hard mind about as easily as roses can penetrate a brick wall.

96. Where the human mind sees great heroes and dangerous villains, Reality sees one mass of equally lost human beings.

97. Only those who honestly admit they are lost are capable of finding themselves.

98. Is the truly sincere person the one who is trying to save the world or the one trying to save himself from himself?

99. Anyone can discover what his life on earth is all about once he chooses self-discovery over self-glory.

100. The jungle will not change, but you can change, so start today with good cheer!

2

The New Land Beyond
the Human Jungle

A class of schoolchildren were on a guided tour of a lighthouse on the coast of Scotland. A lad asked his teacher, "How can ships see the light through a heavy storm?" The teacher explained, "The light can pass through the storm because it is not part of the storm."

It is a provable fact that you can pass untouched through the exterior storms of life. How? Find and live from that real and permanent part of yourself that is not part of the human storm. And how can you do *that?* Collect clues as to the nature of this new and peaceful land beyond the human jungle. Take sentence 138 in this chapter: "Collected knowledge brings into sight the cosmic castle which was formerly beyond our vision." Now suppose you have a problem with someone. What knowledge can begin to carry you safely through the difficulty? This chapter alone contains dozens of guides for this problem. For example, you will learn to look beyond your usual methods for calming a crisis to new and effective techniques. Or, you will see that sex, while a powerful force, comes under the command of a clear mind. Thirdly, you might realize the startling fact that other people are exploiting you in the name of friendship, which sets you free.

The new land is a paradise island growing many fruits of wisdom. Sail for it now.

The New Land Beyond the Human Jungle

101. The secret of celestial success is to let right motives use right ideas for right rewards.

102. We win the opportunity to go beyond ourselves by learning to look beyond ourselves.

103. When emerging from the jungle we find that sex no longer creates problems.

104. Whoever suspects he may be trapped by his own cherished illusions is beginning to break the trap.

105. Remind yourself daily that the way the world goes is not the way you really want to go.

106. God, Truth, Reality, can communicate in total silence as well as with words, so have a silent and receptive mind.

107. A real reward reveals itself every time you see through a false reward, such as flattery.

108. Escape from the human jungle is an inner action, unseen and unapplauded by the jungle inhabitants.

109. Bravely pass through the wilderness within, after which you will reach the colorful meadow within.

110. As we escape the rules of our habitual nature we come under the healthy rules of our cosmic nature.

111. Realize that spiritual sight exists just as definitely as seeing with the eyes.

112. Truth is invisible gold which can be seen

only by those who have developed their cosmic vision.

113. Cosmic insight enables you to know a hundred facts about a person by reading his face.

114. Awareness of how easily life can hit and hurt us is the first course in the cosmic college.

115. We are never required to be important or impressive or needed, but required only to be right.

116. When the words *submission* and *domination* have no place in your life you are out of the jungle.

117. Truth never plays false roles of any kind, which is why people are so surprised when meeting it.

118. Help yourself by thinking about these ideas every possible moment and by creating more thoughtful moments.

119. Each time you question the necessity of a troubled day you weaken the necessity for a troubled day.

120. Ask for anything that is really right and it will begin to travel toward you.

The Miracle Within

121. The inner miracle can happen all right, providing we go into energetic inner action.

122. Simply suspect that you do not consist of your acquired ideas about yourself–and the inner miracle begins.

123. Responsibility for your own cosmic maturity is the only responsibility you have on earth.

124. Right responsibility for yourself *is right responsibility toward others.*

125. Raise your own consciousness even one inch and you perform an act of genuine compassion for others.

126. Consistently use the bit of insight you now have toward self-awakening, and more will be added.

127. Contact with God or Truth or Reality is the same as blending with your own authentic nature.

128. Everyone who has escaped the jungle is aware of his former strange fondness for the jungle's falseness.

129. A daring and helpful question is to ask, "What am I really like inwardly?"

130. It is our awareness of mental boundaries that carries us beyond them.

131. Everyone must decide whether he wants the uncompromising truth or a counterfeit version of truth.

132. Pass through the temporary emptiness of not having the answers and it will be filled with the Answer.

133. Anyone who can be told he is on the wrong path is already approaching the right path.

134. Determine to learn to think rightly toward everything, even if unaware of where it may lead.

135. People who fear to leave their childish ways will always criticize your decision to seek the new nation.

136. Real wisdom consists of recommending the truth to yourself at every opportunity.

137. A real teacher tells you to do things you cannot understand because he can see things you cannot see.

138. Collected knowledge brings into sight the cosmic castle which was formerly beyond our vision.

139. The true view supplies a new kind of thrill that may appear to depart but never does.

140. Dull aches cannot follow us into tomorrow once we learn how to cancel them today.

Teach Yourself the Right Way

141. Everyone is either teaching himself how to wander in the wilderness or how to return home.

142. Your present social condition of any kind can be used as an aid in spiritual progress.

143. To gain real riches you must never ask society to explain the nature of real riches.

144. A cosmically sane man dwelling quietly in society is worth more than a million screamers for reform.

145. You are much stronger than the human jungle, and it is your happy task to realize it.

146. God, Truth, Reality does not want you to be scared of anything, which is why it requests your earnest attention to the healing messages.

147. Either the real can conquer the false or it cannot, but it happens that it can.

148. These facts which at first appear strange and challenging will one day be seen as the only real friends we ever had.

149. You can do something good for yourself

only after seeing that your usual nature can do nothing good for you.

150. These teachings start you in a new direction, and eventually you will see refreshing sights on all sides.

151. Offered truth arouses right feelings in those who already have a seed of truth within themselves.

152. Rescue begins the moment one discovers that *his* truth is not *the* truth.

153. Change what you are, for what you are determines the quality or nonquality of both today and tomorrow.

154. Keeping others in psychological prison is exactly what maintains self-imprisonment.

155. Self-release comes with insight, after which we quietly release others from our demands.

156. Those who have talked themselves into accepting fantasy as fact must now stop talking and begin to listen.

157. We can listen to our mechanical mind or we can listen to something new, and everything depends upon our decision.

158. Your basic objection to society's darkness is correct, but go higher to where it cannot hurt you.

159. The reason a man must awaken is because it is dangerous to sleep, as the man's present life proves.

160. Truth comes as a vague sensing at first, like hearing a familiar voice in the next room but being unable to connect it with a face.

A Higher World Exists

161. It is a provable fact that another world exists above the borders of your usual mind.

162. Ponder simple truths, for example, "Something exists which is higher than our usual desires."

163. Starting now, place your own life ahead of the cunning demands of people who scheme to use you.

164. Using others and being used by others has no place in the life of the enlightened person.

165. Just as the seed contains the undeveloped blossom, so does every individual contain true life ready for development.

166. When even one small part of you takes on the nature of the whole truth you are on the upward trail.

167. First turn away from what you presently see and you will then see wonders you never knew existed.

168. If you do not know what you should be, you should be alert, be aware, be awake.

169. The first step toward practical self-knowledge is to realize that something is dreadfully wrong, and the second step is to sense that all can be made right.

170. We begin to awaken from the nightmare the moment we refuse to continue to call it a lovely dream.

171. These teachings are a new kind of psychic food which provides a unique inner nutrition.

172. Fixed ideas are just fine for building a house or cooking a meal, but are barriers to the inner kingdom.

173. The Road to Reality is traveled successfully by those who once dared to depart from friends who preferred to remain in the Desert of Delusion.

174. Realize that you must know something but never assume that you know what you must know.

175. Do not expect the new world to resemble

the old world and you will enter the new.

176. A sensible question is any question that wants to know what life is really all about.

177. One bridge by which you cross over to self-newness is called *teachability*.

178. One day you will sense that your usual nature is incapable of revealing the Other World, at which point the Other World will begin to reveal itself to you.

179. Strengthen the part of you that wants truth above all else, and watch the happy results.

180. To be in right relationship with others means to be cosmically right within yourself, regardless of how others behave.

Something Beautiful and Intelligent

181. It is beautiful and intelligent to go through each day with the aim to learn more about the higher life.

182. An owl who has escaped the jungle is never again deceived by parrots who call themselves owls.

183. A free man is free because at one point in his life he became willing to hear what he did not want to hear.

184. The aim is to have a cosmic conscience, which is not the same as behavior approved by society, which is hypocrisy.

185. Understand that your personal world is not the entire world and you will perceive the Whole World.

186. When ceasing to think in our usual way we cease to exist in our usual way, and that is the entire secret of self-liberation.

187. Just as a vigorous shake can awaken a sleeping man, a severe crisis, rightly used, can start cosmic awakening.

188. The reason we seek true mental maturity is because immaturity keeps us secretly unhappy.

189. Just to see that you do not presently understand what it means to change inwardly can start that great change.

190. Repeat to yourself, "Whether aware of it or not I am inwardly asleep, but can awaken to true life."

191. Try to realize your need of a totally different viewpoint toward life, which exists as surely as the sun.

192. There is nothing scary about losing the battle against truth, for that defeat is true victory.

193. Though unable to receive truth, a willingness to be able will finally succeed for us.

194. Ordinary thought appears to unite us with Truth, but in fact it separates us.

195. Cosmic consciousness, which is not the same as ordinary thought, unites us with both truth and our own essence.

196. You can define cosmic consciousness as a higher way of seeing life, a way having no negativities.

197. The reward for having a true existence is the departure of the penalties of not having a true existence.

198. The new way can be found, and to review these guides to it is right self-encouragement.

199. Obstacles now blocking self-newness have no permanence, but will finally yield before your right actions.

200. Explore these principles with the zeal of an adventurer who has entered a new and wondrous land.

3

How to Make Your Escape a Pleasure

Imagine yourself strolling down a street and you come to a corner. In one direction you hear a mob shouting and quarreling loudly. In a second direction you hear the crashing noise of industrial machines. But from a third direction comes the sound of beautiful music. Do you have any problem in deciding which way to go? Of course not. There is no struggle with a decision. There is something within you that harmonizes with the music, that makes you want to go toward it.

In this chapter you will hear the pleasurable call to self-harmony. Like the Prodigal Son, the urge to return to the true kingdom can be heard by all who are weary of wandering.

Reflect for a moment. What is more pleasurable than knowing that we are escaping the jittery jungle at last? What is more fun than to toss off the burdens of tension and worry? What is more delightful than to feel ourselves returning to our relaxed real nature?

And remember, the truly pleasurable is also the truly practical. Nothing is more practical than these royal facts. Apply them to every area of daily life and experience healing. Ask them to prove themselves in a personal frustration or a haunting insecurity and they will know what to do and will tell you.

Let this chapter reveal the real meaning of pleasure–the lasting and effortless pleasure of self-wholeness.

How to Make Your Escape a Pleasure

201. Change your direction today, and tomorrow you will not meet the griefs you would have met.

202. When free of pouncing upon ourselves we are also immune to the pouncing of others.

203. Place the practical before the pleasurable and the practical will become the pleasurable.

204. The truly practical person is one who is trying to understand and end his inner warfare.

205. Be glad when useless paths are exposed as useless, for now you can walk the worthwhile path you really want.

206. It should be a positive delight to destroy false rewards in order to find the Real Reward.

207. Wondering whether other people can help you is not a very pleasant way to spend a life.

208. Wondering whether there might be something else is a very pleasant way to start a new life.

209. A man must see that the price he pays for remaining in dreamland is much too high.

210. The one way to stop paying the price is to feel absolutely appalled that you are.

211. It is unnecessary to obey any arising reaction which tells us to act against our true interest.

212. As insight advances you find self-injury and self-accusation occurring less and less.

213. Notice how outer actions cause your inner reactions, then strive for inner independence.

214. By not traveling with the deluded crowd you will not fall when it falls.

215. Realize that all the energy wasted in heartache and regret can be used to generate cosmic light.

216. When truth cuts off our escapes into fantasies, it shows us how much it cares.

217. Perform one right inner action each day and you will see the psychic scenery grow greener.

218. Whether presently realized or not, you can win over every difficulty in life, providing *you are willing to win in a new way.*

219. Winning in a new way consists of seeing that a problem resides in wrong thinking, which cosmic insight can correct.

220. Secret suffering can be understood and it must be understood if it is to come to an end.

Enjoy Great Relief

221. The person who wins over himself enjoys great relief in not having to win over others.

222. These teachings provide a new and pleasant feeling toward oneself based in reality, not imagination.

223. Your essence always knows what is best for you, so recover it by dropping the surface self.

224. You can escape the human jungle by daring to disbelieve society when it talks about love.

225. Society knows as much about authentic love as a jungle beast knows about a rainbow.

226. End the jungle within oneself and the exterior jungle has no more terrors.

227. Thoroughly and enjoyably examine one lesson at a time, having no concern over the next lesson.

228. One purpose of these teachings is to help us to no longer live by the ideas which have caused so much grief.

229. Stop apologizing for yourself and start understanding yourself and see what a difference it makes!

230. It is not cynical to see through the masks of men, but the beginning of real liberty.

231. Walk calmly away from anyone whose manner threatens, "Give me what I demand or I will cause trouble."

232. Allow the inner instructor to guide you

toward the inner treasure.

233. Do not listen to the fear of letting go of yourself and you will soon hear something refreshing.

234. Since you are a different person than you imagine, you have a higher intelligence than you imagine.

235. The artificial self feels surrounded by enemies, while the real self enjoys a pleasant stroll.

236. Egotism is pain, and the only way to end it is to cease to believe that the world revolves around one's petty life.

237. Whether an individual knows it or not there is another way, and it is his true pleasure to know it.

238. A successful day consists of seeing something about yourself in the evening that you did not see in the morning.

239. When a man becomes truthful about his motives he starts to free himself of self-harming motives.

240. While inner work is challenging, it is also cheery, for we are finding what we always wanted to find.

An Astonishing Secret

241. These teachings reveal the astonishing secret of how to be truly valuable to yourself.

242. We need not fear the exposure of a pretense, but should be glad that another chain has fallen.

243. Have a cosmic plan for your life, then watch how earthly plans go smoothly.

244. Unpleasant facts about human nature are not personal problems to those who see them with cosmic insight.

245. It is just as unnecessary to remain with an unpleasant feeling as with an unpleasant person.

246. You cannot stop destructive actions by others, but you can stop your own destructive reactions to them.

247. Anyone who spoils the sleep which we take as consciousness is doing us the favor of our lives.

248. If you want a right feeling, do something right with yourself, for instance, invite rescuing facts.

249. Intelligence is rising when one sees that

human solutions only increase the problem.

250. Each time you consciously risk rejection you add another pearl in your cosmic treasury.

251. Sincere action toward a dim truth will brighten your perception of it.

252. Sincere action is any movement motivated by a wish to see what you do not presently see.

253. Truth's compassion is beautifully apparent when it asks, "What are you doing to help yourself?"

254. Ignore completely what other people want for themselves in this life and want only wholeness for yourself.

255. Right progress consists of an orderly and satisfying release of your own rays of covered light.

256. The truly practical and the truly spiritual are exactly the same thing.

257. Think of the inner path as an interesting adventure, for in fact nothing in life is more interesting.

258. Some people start the path by departing from activities in which they only pretend to have an interest.

259. To reflect about one's confusion is a

healthy and honest act leading to mental clearness.

260. It is possible to think in a winning way toward difficulties, so seek that satisfying way.

Have Cosmic Boldness

261. Be audacious in your effort to see what it is necessary and possible to see.

262. Replace "I have something to fear" with "I have something to learn."

263. Above the shallow pleasures of life which fade away is the permanent pleasure of living who you really are.

264. Fear of inner discovery makes as much sense as fearing to leave a sinking ship for the voyage to solid land.

265. Realize that the false self makes problems out of everything, then ask whether you want its company.

266. True pleasure consists of the steady replacement of the imaginary self by the real self.

267. Truth is absolutely delighted with anyone who walks toward it while simply wondering what it is all about.

268. Sincerity supplies the two rewards of simplifying your task and making it enjoyable.

269. The last thing falsehood wants you to do is question it, so question it.

270. What a relief to discover we need not do all those things we thought were our social duties!

271. See beyond self-descriptive labels, such as wife or businessman or winner or loser, and see yourself as a free human being without labels.

272. Since problems arise from psychic hypnosis it makes perfect sense to probe the nature of this hypnosis.

273. To rescue yourself you must first stop trying to save the world–which does not want to be saved anyway.

274. Everyone who lives on the mountain peak once saw the folly of trying to save others before saving himself.

275. The secret of progress is to stop alternating between mistake and guilt to start alternating between mistake and learning.

276. Will you trust a religion or philosophy that does not produce a truly poised and decent human being?

277. When really turning toward truth, you will feel truth turning toward you.

278. Have confidence in these teachings by seeing how accurately they describe human lunacy.

279. Today, take a long step forward by no longer permitting negative people to influence you in any way.

280. Delusions end only when the deluded realizes that his supposed rewards were really punishments.

An Incredible Reality

281. It is an incredible reality that all we are asked to give up is whatever is making us unhappy.

282. Become very curious that there might be much more to life than you now see, for there is.

283. Truth cordially welcomes anyone who searches for it, no matter how awkward the search.

284. Use mental dispute rightly by seeing that life's answers can never be found in dispute.

285. The answers which exist above dispute reveal themselves to anyone who willingly drops dispute.

286. A main reason for pursuing these facts is that they supply new personal qualities.

287. The last thought that should occupy your mind is whether or not other people want to accompany you on the upward path.

288. The reason we must break out of ourselves is that it is so painful to live with ourselves.

289. Taking the initiative toward self-change arouses objections from the old ways, which is exactly why we should take it.

290. Think deeply about the fact that you can learn to not be your own unhappy states.

291. Beware of those who use your fears to exploit you, for the human jungle is thick with such people.

292. Reach beyond your usual thinking for the right answers and you will find them.

293. As sure as sunshine, a new world exists within you, having a new kind of delight.

294. A sleeping mind reacts from its confusion, while an awakened mind understands from its clearness.

295. You are now learning to walk down a single path instead of many frustrating and contradictory paths.

296. The quality of a life can be raised solely by uplifting the quality of the mind.

297. As false thrills fade before self-insight, new and true inspirations take their place.

298. A part of you senses the trueness and the decency of these teachings, so release that part fully.

299. Take self-rescue seriously, which will enable you to take everything else lightly.

300. Think of the new pleasure it will be to go beyond yourself and live beyond yourself!

4

Discover Real Safety
and Security

A party of campers found themselves in a dry, unpleasant and hazardous area near the base of a mountain. Observing their dissatisfaction, an experienced camper strolled over to offer some practical advice. "If you want a safe and beautiful spot," he said, "drive higher up the mountain."

Go higher. In just those two words you have a wealth of information and inspiration.

There are two cosmic laws which every

seeker should learn and ponder: 1. We live a safe or a hazardous life according to the inner level we occupy. 2. By raising the quality of our thoughts and feelings we arrive at the level of authentic safety and security.

Perhaps you know men and women who constantly attract grief and misfortune. Think of just one of them, maybe a relative or friend. Notice how this person thinks and feels and acts. Try to see the connection between the quality or nonquality of his psychic system and what happens to him. See how his inner level attracts people and events on the same level. Conclude that like attracts like.

The secret is out. A sincere and persistent attempt to think and feel right lifts us to the lofty level we really want to occupy. The secret is now yours. Use it for real safety and security, starting with the next lessons.

Discover Real Safety and Security

301. Safety and security change from mere words to personal realities as these facts operate within.

302. When nothing seems to work it is simply because we have not yet turned to Reality, which alone can work.

303. If you can trust a tiger to guide you safely out of the jungle you can also trust society for safety.

304. It is impossible to be disappointed when depending upon higher knowledge for guidance.

305. Ponder the refreshment of having a new and a pleasant relationship with yourself.

306. When we stumble it is simply because we called something light that was not light at all.

307. Realize that these higher facts enable you to escape the human jungle while living in the middle of it.

308. Your escape is real, inner, invisible, having no quarrel with the human jungle because you are no longer part of it.

309. Our real escape begins the moment we no longer evade the fact that we do not know ourselves.

310. There is a part of you which does not fear inner or outer conflict, which you are now developing.

311. When living from our real nature, we never

fear that others may see through us.

312. Correctly tell yourself how to live and no one will dare to toss foolish advice at you.

313. Realize that only the imaginary world can be hurt, for that sets the foundation for the real World.

314. Religious ideas cannot supply inner security any more than a bread label can satisfy hunger.

315. When your ideas insist you are safe, but you feel scared, your feelings are telling the truth.

316. Right ideas are the first steps toward the inner mansion, but they are not the mansion itself.

317. The quality of your life will be the same as the quality of your self-insight.

318. The sooner we take the cosmic medicine the sooner we can stop suffering from ourselves.

319. If you are quite sure that nothing can lift your heavy spirit you simply do not see what can be seen.

320. The loss you feel is the loss of yourself, but happily, you can find yourself.

A Safe Place

321. Whether you know it or not, truth knows it is leading you toward a safe place, so why not confidently follow?

322. Lift your spirit just one degree above worldly affairs and you will feel release from worldly conflict.

323. Anyone who thinks society's social schemes can banish anxiety should ask why they have not done so.

324. We react to events as we do because we know no other way, but a superior way awaits our discovery.

325. Separate what is your own from what is not your own, and insecurity is not your own.

326. Inward clearness knows exactly how to make the outward life go smoothly.

327. When the individual is right his circumstances are right, for he is his own circumstances.

328. These teachings turn hazardous mental states into safe mental conditions.

329. When events do not obey your desires, know that *real peace does not depend upon them doing so.*

330. By psychic law we get what we actually give, which may be quite different from what we say we give.

331. The first faint realization that one is his own trap has already weakened the trap.

332. Feeling secure because of favorable conditions is like feeling safe while sleeping next to a cliff.

333. Only the security of knowing yourself as One with the All can stand against changing conditions.

334. Consciously risk the loss of something before losing it and you will lose the fear of losing it.

335. The solution is a secret only as long as we buy dreams instead of realities.

336. The sooner we stop playing little games with truth the sooner we will have what we need.

337. Have no fear of coming to an end of yourself, for then you will know who you really are, which is peace at last.

338. The world we struggle with is not the only world existing for us.

339. We can vainly try to hold falsehood or we can wisely let truth hold us.

340. The only way to win over this deluded world is to live inwardly above its hysteria.

A Higher Good for You

341. These teachings supply a higher definition of doing good things for yourself.

342. Everything begins to go right the instant one realizes he is not the surface personality he assumed he was.

343. It is necessary to see through ourselves, and any resistance to it maintains the slippery way.

344. Confusion in ourselves or in others is strengthened by fearing it, so fear not.

345. Catch yourself wandering in the past or future and leap back to the liberty of now.

346. Walk into a situation consciously and you will be able to walk out of it harmlessly.

347. When raising your level of cosmic comprehension you also raise your value to yourself.

348. A foremost peril in life is to close the eyes to human nature as it is in fact.

349. New safety begins the moment you suspect that the human condition is much worse than you imagined.

350. Rushing emotions have no more real power to sweep you away than a tiny brook can move a boulder.

351. Believing what we want to believe attracts what we do not want to attract.

352. A shocking experience is simply a lesson in seeing that we were asleep while dreaming we were awake, for reality is shockless.

353. A negative nature cannot be reformed, but it can be replaced by a cosmic nature.

354. True cheerfulness is not a result of exciting thoughts or favorable events, but is a poise resting upon its own Oneness with the Universe.

355. Learn what it means to hold out the lamp of consciousness before your daily path.

356. The world has no power whatever to enter and hurt the mansion within.

357. Real humility helps, and real humility consists of seeing honestly that our usual ideas lead nowhere.

358. We lose our petty plans with fear and trembling, only to win the cosmic plan with wonder and delight.

359. Truth alone is truthful toward us, which means that truth alone can help us.

360. Any spiritual remedy which must be fearfully and angrily defended is no remedy at all.

The Answer to All Problems

361. The cause of every problem is lack of insight into your real nature, so now you know the solution to every problem.

362. Everyone you meet gives you exactly what he is, so wisely discover what he is.

363. Reflect upon the powerful cosmic fact that the absence of inner enemies means the absence of outer enemies.

364. Cosmic insight can see how things will turn out and therefore never starts anything that would end badly.

365. If you wish to know why self-insight is valuable, it is because harmony is better than conflict.

366. When really knowing the truth, we never need to anxiously convince ourselves that we know.

367. If feeling that you are not where you ought to be, follow it all the way to where you should be.

368. The plain fact is that you need not tolerate

a mind that tries to bother you.

369. Each time you sincerely want to know why you suffer so much you open the gate to eventual comprehension.

370. The only thing you need in any situation is for your mind to think clearly and intelligently toward it.

371. Mingle with right thoughts and you will know what people to mingle with for right relationships.

372. Only those who really want to know will listen persistently to those who really know.

373. You were not placed in the world to wander aimlessly, but placed to discover the Cosmic Castle.

374. Fearing to lose our present wrong values is like fearing the loss of physical illness.

375. We are under social pressures only to the degree that we are not under cosmic influences.

376. Become aware of useless thinking and acting, and their burdens will fall off your life.

377. Notice the fear of losing a present security, then let these principles conquer the fear.

378. Even while frantically seeking security in exterior sources, try to remember that real stability is found only in self-unity attained through self-knowledge.

379. A safe relationship with yourself guarantees a safe relationship with others.

380. A safe relationship with yourself is the result of true spiritual rebirth.

Win a New View

381. The whole idea is to change your psychic position to win a new view of surrounding life.

382. It is not risky at all to risk the dislike of someone in favor of being and acting what is true.

383. Timid withdrawal into oneself as a means of feeling safe is the very cause of insecurity.

384. Refuse absolutely to let careless mistakes torture your mind and you will learn to rise above them.

385. When the lower earnestly seeks the higher, the higher promptly allows itself to be found.

386. Live these teachings and live a secret life untouched by silly society.

387. At this moment millions of human beings are sad and confused through lack of higher wisdom, but you need not be one of them.

388. The only true and strong reassurance on earth comes from your own recovered essence.

389. Anything that jolts your fixed position is trying to give you a new position which cannot be jolted.

390. Live from essence instead of surface personality, for your essence alone is free from threat and damage.

391. Cosmic Power takes full responsibility for those who first take full responsibility for themselves.

392. An understood fear ceases to be a burden, for instance, the fear of being disliked, when understood, ceases to be a burden.

393. Self-leadership based in essence is the only kind of accurate and satisfying leadership.

394. Be fully aware of what you do not want in your life and soon you will see what you do want.

395. Blows to our sense of security *taken consciously* will make us so secure we need never think about security.

396. Your daily actions will be as accurate as your level of being permits.

397. We are never really betrayed by other people, but are betrayed only by our own refusal to listen, to learn, to see.

398. Anything that forces us to face our actual confusion is always a friend, never an enemy, and we will eventually rea!ize this.

399. Do not be dismayed when seeing you are not who you thought you were, for now you will know who you really are.

400. The real riches found by your own studies become part of your very nature and therefore can never be lost.

5

You Can Succeed with Cosmic Confidence

Rain falls only once every several years in parts of the immense Sahara Desert in North Africa. Yet when rain finally falls, sleeping seeds in the earth awaken to create colorful scenery. The seeds had always contained their own self-power and self-confidence, and waited only for the time for creative expression of their inner naturalness.

No matter how long we have been asleep to our natural confidence, receptivity to higher truths can awaken us. You, reader, can personally experience this.

Exactly what is natural confidence? Our real nature knows without even thinking about it. And we can find the answer for ourselves by first asking the interesting question, "What is *artificial* confidence?" Ah! *That* we know! We see it all around us in this shaky society. Bluff and bluster are certainly examples of false courage. Fearful defensiveness tries to pass itself off as strength, but is really a lack of inner poise.

One may wonder what awareness of the artificial has to do with finding the natural. A vital principle makes this clear: *Deep awareness of the false makes us want to drop it, leaving room for the true.* It is like a sculptor who chips away at a block of marble to reveal the figure within.

Keep this principle in mind as you proceed with this chapter.

You Can Succeed with Cosmic Confidence

401. Cosmic confidence arises from a clear knowledge that you are part of the Universal Whole.

402. There are a thousand good reasons why you should seek cosmic courage and not one reason why you should not.

403. One good reason for seeking celestial confidence is that it alone can conquer concealed frustration.

404. In back of every unhappy feeling is a power which can be released to end the feeling.

405. You need not know in advance where the Path is leading you, for *it* knows and will lead you accurately.

406. Agony has no life of its own, but is kept in motion only by our own unawareness of this great fact.

407. Anything that frightens you in your search for truth is false, so ignore it and march forward.

408. There is no need whatever to permit outer voices and influences to lead you astray.

409. Understand yourself and you understand the universe, for you are a representative of the universe.

410. You are given the inner task because it is possible for you to succeed in it.

411. Force yourself out of your usual world on Monday, which will be followed by bewilderment on Tuesday, and by certainty on Wednesday.

412. Know that these facts are the true heroes who rescue us from the prison of misunderstanding.

413. These are not merely religious or philosophic ideas, but practical facts which create an inward new world.

414. When still living from the invented identity, all talk about confidence is empty words.

415. An authentic teacher knows all about your hidden powers and helps their development.

416. Personal understanding opens slowly or swiftly according to one's own degree of self-reliance and self-responsibility.

417. A conscious act is one in which there are no present doubts and no future regrets.

418. When you are quite sure you cannot be brave for yourself, you will attract cosmic bravery.

419. Truth is the conqueror of weakness, so what alliance will give you real strength?

420. False confidence depends anxiously upon something exterior, while real courage rests quietly in itself.

How to Command Conditions

421. You command a condition by having no negative attitudes toward it.

422. Harmful influences and harmful events cannot capture anyone with cosmic confidence.

423. Think of a problem that attacks your mind, then know that these ideas can free your mind.

424. You need have no doubts at all about the rightness and the power of the plans you are now absorbing.

425. Spiritual valor consists of getting up after a fall without looking around to see who witnessed your disgrace.

426. By bearing your own problems you develop strength to end your own problems.

427. Cosmic confidence grows with the simple realization that truth exists–which few people really realize.

428. A real teacher helps you to find your cosmic certainty, while a false teacher simply exploits you.

429. Truth knows exactly what you should do with yourself all day long, so why not let it tell you?

430. Mistaking dependency for personal strength is a major cause of shock and distress.

431. Shallow human confidence can be shaken with the smallest frown, but cosmic confidence has independent strength.

432. A form of false confidence which crumbles quickly is a hope that certain things will remain as they are.

433. Cosmic valor never falters, for it arises from God, Truth, Reality, not from human thought.

434. When finding the real riches of your cosmic nature, you will find them inexhaustible.

435. The royal road to self-newness opens to anyone who patiently studies what it means to change his viewpoints.

436. You know what Reality knows by blending into Oneness with Reality.

437. You can learn to walk past discouragement just as easily as you walk past a supposedly haunted house.

438. Self-unity is the same as rightness, and rightness is the same as permanent strength and effortless action.

439. Real competence in human affairs

becomes possible only after the attainment of cosmic competence.

440. If your present way does not supply self-command it makes perfect sense to locate the Other Way.

Release Real Confidence

441. Your true nature will be confident for you, so do your part of releasing it.

442. Invisible powers are with you from the start of your journey, as you will eventually see.

443. It is necessary to lose confidence in shallow human nature in order to win cosmic confidence.

444. Have no hesitation in losing confidence in artificial people, for it opens the door to unshakeable poise.

445. Exhaust your own strength and cosmic power will come, but you must do it, not think it.

446. Cease to believe in the power of the imaginary self, and watch the arrival of cosmic strength.

447. The more you ask from yourself in the inner task the more you will get from yourself.

448. Naturalness thinks and feels and acts in quiet and commanding confidence.

449. Have no fear in not depending upon your present strengths, for that opens the door to higher powers.

450. Live from recovered essence, not imaginary identity, and self-doubt vanishes forever.

451. The artificial self is helpless, which should urge us to rise to the level of cosmic competence.

452. We need not hide anything from Truth, for it never condemns us, but wishes only to help.

453. You will win inner victory sooner by not wasting energy in wondering whether it is possible.

454. If your life is in chaos you are at the perfect starting point for seeking peaceful reality.

455. People fear to be without something to think about, but the end of this compulsion assures mental liberty.

456. Receiving facts that part of us does not want to receive is a sign of cosmic courage.

457. Learn to relax the mind, for a mind at ease flows with its full resources.

458. No one needs to remain timid any more than he needs to remain in a desolate desert.

459. Realize that higher forces try to reach and help you, so let them succeed by dropping mental walls.

460. Energy spent in feeling sad over inability should be spent in creating ability.

You Can Change Direction

461. Truth changes your direction, so no mistake in your life ever sets a permanent course.

462. We collapse because we are shakily supported by *mere ideas about self-strength* instead of living from real strength.

463. Whatever you are asked to do for yourself you are quite capable of doing for yourself.

464. Dare to rely upon your own hidden powers even when you cannot see them.

465. When trusting yourself remember that you are trusting your real nature, not your usual self.

466. Bravely enter into self-doubt and one day imaginary confidence will give way to cosmic confidence.

467. Courage to face oneself develops swiftly by the persistent practice of facing oneself.

468. If you want the jewels hidden in the dragon's cave, have the courage to enter the cave.

469. Why depend upon the supposed courage of others when you can have your own real certainty?

470. The one way to invite real strength is to stop inviting the artificial strength of surface personality.

471. Right self-encouragement consists simply of receiving the facts about life, whether pleasant or unpleasant.

472. True confidence comes from self-insight, while false confidence comes from imitative ideas.

473. Each time you are consciously strong for another person you increase your own strength.

474. The supreme answer is within you, just as the melody is somewhere within the piano.

475. A truly brave act is to cut off your own escapes into delusion and deception.

476. Have confidence toward inner success, for all the good powers in the universe will help you.

477. It is great encouragement to realize that truth will not tolerate human deception.

478. Dedication develops invisible forces, which one day will become visible to inner sight.

479. True explanations of life are alone capable of support in daily doubts and shakings.

480. Aid from cosmic confidence is the only kind of aid that will never fail you.

A Relaxing Idea

481. It is both relaxing and empowering to realize you need only continue with the inner adventure in spite of all difficulties.

482. Just as darkness cannot put out a candle, evil has no real power over goodness.

483. If feeling weak along the path revive yourself with that fine power called *endurance*.

484. Real courage consists of repeatedly leaping beyond surface personality even while fearing to do so, until all fear vanishes.

485. The secret of inner wealth is to meet an old condition in a new way, for example, try to understand a situation instead of agitating over it.

486. Refuse to give attention to senseless and haunting thoughts and they will get discouraged and depart.

487. It is a happy day when one realizes he simple cannot afford to continue with his false confidence.

488. Unconscious smugness is a form of false confidence which must be dropped if we are to develop inwardly.

489. Make everyday decisions consciously, for this builds strength to make life-transforming decisions.

490. Your past can be changed in an astonishing way by seeing it with these higher truths.

491. When puzzled or discouraged, return to these ideas, for that act by itself adds strength.

492. Weakness is nothing but a temporary separation of the individual from his natural strength.

493. One day you will see that being yourself is the same as supplying yourself with endless strength and poise.

494. We have lost contact with our natural confidence, but can start today to restore it.

495. Distress is simply a wrong reaction which fades as we practice the right reaction of cosmic consciousness.

496. The vital fact is not the severe inner storm but the fact that you can advance through it.

497. Develop a new inner efficiency and it will extend itself to efficiency in exterior affairs.

498. When not knowing what to do with yourself, the perfect activity is the acquisition of self-knowledge.

499. You have a right side, and your real pleasure is to place yourself on that side.

500. These teachings unlock the doors leading to the refreshing life you really want.

6

How to Avoid Traps in the Human Jungle

A perplexed inquirer complained to a wise man, "I am at the mercy of every unexpected event and involvement. What can I do?" Explained the wise man, "Involve yourself with inner command and all other involvements will come under your command."

A mind operating with cosmic command is never at the mercy of anyone or anything. You can see why. Cosmic vision sees things as they are, and therefore can never be deceived or exploited.

Do you know Arthur Schopenhauer? He was a German philosopher with the eye of a hawk and a pen like a sword. He knew more about human nature than a convention of psychiatrists. Listen to his blunt advice for avoiding human traps:

"You will see that, in dealing with fools and blockheads, there is only one way of showing your intelligence–by having nothing to do with them. That means, of course, that when you go into society, you may now and then feel like a good dancer who gets an invitation to a ball, and on arriving, finds that everyone is lame–with whom is he to dance?"

Cynical statements? Maybe. Accurate observations? Certainly. We can rise above cynicism, for to be cynical is to be still chained to the follies of other people. It is quite possible to see people as they are without shaking with self-reference.

Where the uncompromising Arthur Schopenhauer stops, the following points take over.

How to Avoid Traps in the Human Jungle

501. The question is, who will protect you from the people who are supposed to protect you?

502. The only person who can help you escape is one who has himself escaped, so think deeply about this.

503. Departing from our usual ideas is as refreshing as leaving a familiar but noisy big city.

504. Trying to do good without knowing the nature of real goodness creates resentment and weariness.

505. Those who have escaped the human jungle realize how little they could be told at one time.

506. Ignorant people remain ignorant because they have a secret agreement to call each other intelligent.

507. To win real rewards we must firmly decline the deceptive rewards offered by society.

508. The gullible believe that a hawk is a dove and then wonder why they get hurt.

509. Falsehood has thousands of dangerous notions, while truth has but one answer, which is, "Find your real self."

510. As long as a person imagines he knows what he is doing with himself, he does not know.

511. When really seeing what it means to hurt ourselves, we no longer do it.

512. Lost people try to impose a sense of guilt upon others, but sane people refuse it.

513. When we see the real reason for doing something, we end our slavery toward the invented reason.

514. The truly healthy man, having power over himself, has no craving to dominate others.

515. The desire to have power over others places one under the power of others.

516. Tricky thoughts can deceive us into thinking we know what is best for us, so see through these harmful ideas.

517. False strength can be recognized by the way it trembles when our small and self-centered world is threatened.

518. Misfortunes happen to us which need not happen, and these teachings reveal the escape.

519. If clawed by human tigers it is simply because we unnecessarily inhabit the psychic jungle.

520. Gullibility consists of not seeing people as

they really are until they have taken all they can from you.

A Helpful Question

521. When someone insists upon arguing, ask him, "Why do you feel it necessary to have an enemy?"

522. Preventing anyone from learning from his own mistake is a great mistake.

523. If you want a welcome having no hidden traps, accept the honest welcome of these teachings.

524. If we can mix water with fire we can also mix truthful ideas with foolish notions.

525. A major aim is to stop the invented personality from masquerading as the real person.

526. If we get into trouble we can be sure it was caused by the invented personality.

527. Remind yourself a thousand times that a cruel man who says he is sorry has not changed his nature.

528. Wars will not stop as long as people pretend that war is something apart from their own warring natures.

529. We reject the true and accept the false because we imagine we already know the difference between them.

530. Curiously, we believe that we need the harmful, but the instructive light brings release and relief.

531. If you have been left out of society's excitement, be glad, for now you will not have to pay the penalty.

532. Human authority consists of men lost in the storm who assume solemn facial expressions and tell others how to escape the storm.

533. Hoping for something good to come is unnecessary self-torment, for all goodness is now available to your perception.

534. One thing that discourages anxiety from attacking is your calm refusal to fear it.

535. Self-betrayal is exactly the same thing as consenting to betrayal by other people.

536. Allowing emotions to swamp the mind is like pouring molasses on a needed road map.

537. Most people who say they trust God usually trust their *acquired ideas about God.*

538. Only the surface mind feels lost and lonely, which is sufficient reason for rising above it.

539. Be aware of how human nature declares, "I want the glory but you do the work."

540. When habitual thinking talks about love it has no love at all, for habitual thinking conceals cunning self-interest.

Your Cosmic College

541. Let others continue to be busy doing nothing, while you wisely attend cosmic college.

542. One self-liberating insight is to see that people can behave no higher than their own cosmic level.

543. If you can come to a teacher on your own terms you are not meeting a real teacher.

544. Try to see that *thinking* we understand a certain thing is not at all the same as actually understanding it.

545. Just as a shadow is the result of blocked light, human darkness is caused by blocked cosmic sunshine.

546. We must never forget that wrong ideas about life and boredom always go together.

547. Let other people tell you what you want and they will end up telling you what they want.

548. When seeking, take care to not simply switch from one wrong trail to another.

549. Untrue ideas are like enemy soldiers disguised as friends who subtly work at the downfall of the psychic fortress.

550. If you feel that life is hostile toward you, and you study these ideas, the hostility will vanish.

551. A refusal to see what is truly good for us separates us from what is truly good for us.

552. It sounds too simple to say that lack of self-insight causes our grief, but that is the plain fact.

553. Rescue is available to all who listen, but how many people do you know who want to listen?

554. What deluded society insists is right for you is precisely what is wrong for you.

555. When anyone tells you how to live your life, quietly observe what the advice has done for the advisor.

556. Assume that people will tell you what they know you want to hear and you will seldom be wrong.

557. False teachings allow you to remain as you

are while letting you imagine you have changed.

558. Asking for help but secretly wanting our own way is like buying a lantern but refusing to light it.

559. Truth never enters a room filled with people whose chief talent is to chatter about social service.

560. Weak people who drag you down will always claim to be strong people trying to lift you up.

An Authentic Class

561. One value of an authentic class is what you are *not* given, for example, you are not given nonsense masquerading as help.

562. We attract negative people and events because we wrongly and unconsciously value them.

563. Refuse to play the roles that people try to cast you in–for their benefit.

564. Do not discuss these celestial inspirations with those whose great aim in life is to win power or popularity.

565. Never eagerly pounce on an event in order to feel a thrill, instead, calmly gain insight into the event.

566. If your search is very diligent you will one day meet a teacher who will not deceive you.

567. Hostility sent toward another person returns instantly to injure the sender.

568. A man is punished only by the level he occupies, as when deceit deceives the deceitful.

569. What is called worship or meditation is often nothing but an evasion of personal responsibility for self-awakening.

570. When someone declares he wants to serve you, try to see where he wants power to bully you.

571. Today, try to see just one human invitation that is really a cunning trap.

572. If social or religious organizations can drink water for you, they can also save you.

573. It takes no courage to cling to acquired beliefs, but takes real courage to abandon them.

574. To the exact degree that we tolerate our own nonsense we must suffer from the nonsense of others.

575. When seeing a distressed person, never forget that you may be his next target.

576. Those who gain a false identity out of hoaxing and hurting you are no friends of yours.

577. Everyone who refuses truth and decency will always lie about the reasons for his refusal.

578. You can end half your troubles immediately by no longer permitting people to tell you what you want.

579. Realize that feeling helpless and deserted is a false feeling, never your real condition.

580. People unwisely prefer society's syrup, which explains why they are not cured by cosmic medicine.

Follow Your Higher Law

581. Follow the higher law within which knows what is right and it will lead you out of the jungle.

582. When knowing what is right for your life you are not burdened with false concern over the life of others.

583. When permitting other people to think for us, we cannot complain if they think us into disaster.

584. A foremost cause of conflict and confusion is the attempt to behave the way society insists you *should* behave.

585. You should behave in any way that leads to independent command of your own life.

586. There is no way to seek the rewards offered by an unwell society without also seeking its punishments.

587. Let resistance before truth collapse and you will never again collapse before life.

588. When someone tells you he knows the truth, you should watch his face carefully when his claim is rejected.

589. As fear fades through insight into our real nature we cease to attract fearful things.

590. Wisely explain your own behavior to yourself and you are free of anyone who demands that you explain yourself.

591. Entertainment disguised as spiritual instruction keeps many in the human jungle.

592. When a man proudly tells you the kind of person he is, he is telling you the kind of person he is not.

593. Think often of the fact that no man or woman is what he or she appears to be.

594. If people are unable to behave properly in your company, do not give them your company.

595. Detect the private thoughts of anyone

who says he wants to help you, then see whether you still want his help.

596. Realize that surface personality has no interest in anything which might disturb its darling delusions.

597. Sufferers wrongly think they will feel empty without their pain, and so resist Reality's offered cure.

598. If other people tell you what to do it is only because you have not as yet told yourself what to do.

599. The sheep is lost only because of failure to turn in the direction of the shepherd.

600. If you want a way of life having no hidden traps, it exists within your own real nature.

7

Save Years of Search
with these Facts

A famous philosopher was asked by his students, "Why do we behave as we do?" Holding up a clock, the teacher explained, "It is like the inner works of this clock. Understand its hidden parts and you see why its exterior parts move as they do."

The lesson is this: Self-knowledge is the great power by which we comprehend and control our lives.

And the power by which we save years of weary search.

Save Years of Search with these Facts

Here are typical stages in an individual's progress toward the light. 1. At first, he is indifferent toward the truth, for his exciting daily activities keep him distracted from his anxiety. 2. A dawning awareness of his suffering causes him to seek help. 3. He is bewildered and agitated by the great number of organizations which claim to know the answers. 4. He falls into their trapping follies for a period of time, for he does not know what else to do. 5. Courageously realizing that they have nothing real to give him, he begins to search within and to think for himself. 6. His developing consciousness leads him to authentic teachings, perhaps in books or at lectures. 7. He finally reaches a preliminary stage where his own nature becomes his own light, after which he spends his days brightening that light.

The following one hundred principles were designed for your swift progress toward the light.

Save Years of Search
with these Facts

601. Sex, like every other human feature, comes under command as these teachings are absorbed.

602. A rescuing idea is one that disagrees with your habitual nature but which agrees with Truth.

603. Challenging one wrong assumption is a more heroic deed than the conquest.

604. Clear your mind of unnecessary thoughts, and in that new clearness and power you will be astonished at the great number of unnecessary thoughts you once believed necessary.

605. Learn to love new and strange and unfamiliar conditions which force you to explore and discover.

606. What blocks our ascent to the next higher level is the assumption that we are already up there.

607. What we imagine is our power is not power at all, while what we cannot imagine–Truth–is our actual power.

608. You are not required to sacrifice anything but imaginations masquerading as realities.

609. One value of self-observation and self-knowledge is to see who you are *not*.

Save Years of Search with these Facts

610. Discover who you are not, and you are not someone who has to prove who you are.

611. A great surprise and victory in life is to see we were mechanical while calling it conscious behavior.

612. We can be sure we are in dreamland when we resent anything that tries to wake us up.

613. Encourage the awakening of the one part of you that suspects it is dreaming instead of living.

614. See human nonsense *as* nonsense and save years of trying to make sense out of it.

615. There is no way to drop harmful nonsense as long as vanity calls it wisdom.

616. The question is, how can we see that we do not really know what we pretend and insist we know?

617. Anyone who sees he is merely playing the role of self-command has a chance to really command.

618. What happens inside you, not outside, is what needs attention and examination.

619. Change the inner and you change the outer, for the inner and outer are the same.

620. It is a true miracle when a man finally sees

himself as his only opposition.

How to Brighten Tomorrow

621. The guaranteed way to do better tomorrow is to do everything today consciously.

622. Hurt feelings are simply a device of Reality to inform us we are not listening to its wisdom.

623. No one can be helped until he listens to something higher than himself, and no one listens until seeing the need to listen.

624. Playing with words about the spiritual life is not the same as bravely exploring one's inner nature, which alone can build a spiritual life.

625. There is no way to break the chain of troubles without taking personal responsibility for them.

626. Do not try to understand life with your usual kinds of thoughts, for that increases understanding.

627. Seeing our helplessness is just fine as long as it means to see the uselessness of our usual ways.

628. Self-investigation is the method by which

we free ourselves of unconscious self-centeredness.

629. When understanding another person's problem you help him correctly, even though there is nothing you can do about it.

630. The wise seeker uses discouragement as a signal to seek all the harder!

631. Trying to convince ourselves that we are right prevents higher facts from making us right.

632. The only right start toward an understanding of human nature is an admission of a lack of present understanding.

633. A sour apple tree deceives only those who admire the blossoms without tasting the fruit.

634. By seeing human evil seriously in the right way we will finally not take it seriously at all.

635. Seeing evil in the right way is to see it has no power except as we wrongly credit it with power.

636. We cease to credit power to evil by seeing that its pretty packages are empty.

637. When really knowing who you are, you will finally know the answer to the question, "What is truth?"

638. A person radiates what he really is, not

what he imagines he is, and attracts what he radiates.

639. Drop your despair over finding the answers to life and you will find them.

640. Really know what you are like and you will really know what others are like.

Suffering is a Gigantic Hoax

641. Try to see that suffering is a gigantic hoax which cosmic facts can expose.

642. The certain remedy for dull and repetitious days is to live from these esoteric wisdoms.

643. Right answers come when we ask our questions with right attitudes, such as a yearning to know.

644. A man who possesses real gold never bargains over it, which means that truth never compromises with dark human nature.

645. Light never battles darkness, so whenever you see a fight it is always between two dark forces.

646. Take disturbance as an awakening sign that you misunderstand something you assumed you understood.

647. The reason we should abandon falsehood is simply because it is so dangerous to us.

648. A man can insist all day long that his leaky boat is solid, but he will still sink.

649. Unhappiness persists because of the refusal to risk the ruin of the familiar but false ideas.

650. Spiritual studies proceed properly only when including the touchy topic of human hypocrisy.

651. You will not fumble in vain if you fumble in the task of finding your real nature.

652. Regrets at losing social or financial opportunities are both delusion and needless pain.

653. We can be practical and economical in everyday things only by living from higher facts.

654. A secret and cunning fondness for sad circumstances will surely keep them around.

655. Any wish to appear scholarly in the eyes of the public will immediately cut off our opportunity to be sensible.

656. Pretense is never able to admit it is pretense, so an honest part of us must go to work.

657. Chaos persists only because we insist upon living with personal beliefs instead of with cosmic insight.

658. Notice that some of these ideas impress the mind with health, while others impress the emotions.

659. The one way to have something worthwhile to do with your life is to courageously see that you presently have nothing worthwhile.

660. The truly valuable can be defined as that which does not contribute to our false need for ego-gratification.

Walk with Lightness

661. We walk with new lightness when finally seeing that *it is not necessary to pretend to know.*

662. Doing good to someone in order to reduce self-guilt will only ruin things for both of you.

663. Truth prevails in those who were once shocked at seeing they knew nothing about truth.

664. We start the upward path by seeing deeply that our earlier actions were not starts but evasions.

665. The intimidating tricks someone plays on you are the same tricks he most fears might be played on him.

Save Years of Search with these Facts

666. To be afraid of a hostile person makes as much sense as fearing an angry ape in the zoo.
667. We find the light only after total defeat of our attempts to deceive and outwit it.
668. The quality of human life is raised each time an individual reflects, "Maybe I am the problem."
669. The man who really sees his mistake today does not repeat it tomorrow.
670. The stronger the truth given to anyone the stronger will be his positive or negative reaction.
671. Just as weeds absorb water needed by flowers, we waste psychic energy needed for cosmic blossoming.
672. Reclaim your psychic energy by not resisting the vital powers which want to make everything right.
673. If you wish to know the truth you must dare the displeasure of false teachers.
674. Really see the lessons in unhappy experiences and watch how experiences become pleasant.
675. Your wish to escape society's confusion is good, so start by studying your own confusion.

676. Any avoidance of personal darkness, no matter how noble it appears, is an avoidance of light.

677. Trash can be made to look like treasure, but it can never be made to feel like treasure.

678. A good memory of religious ideas is not the same as a good inner nature, but many think so.

679. Hearing these ideas without acting upon them is like buying an airplane but leaving it on the ground.

680. You get something real from an event when there is no tense thought about getting or not getting something.

Help Wishes to Reach You

681. Celestial inspirations are always descending, but our thick attitudes prevent them from reaching the spirit.

682. A sincere question is one in which the answer is more important than the small thrill of asking the question.

683. All attempts to solve the outer problem will fail until we first succeed in solving the inner problem.

684. The only person responsible for a wanderer is the wanderer himself.

685. The truly spiritual person has no need to appear religious before other people.

686. Do you think that tense defense can ever be part of someone who really knows?

687. Unconscious resistance to the rescuing truth must be made conscious, and the best time to do it is now.

688. If your search for help draws you to a group where you remain comfortable, you are in a wrong place.

689. If you cannot change life into what you want you can always change yourself into what you want.

690. If life does not taste right it is simply because we are still dining on familiar but wrong ideas.

691. Only wholeness can see the difference between wholeness and abnormality.

692. Neurotic guilt must be understood and ended, otherwise individual and mass destruction will continue.

693. Feelings of release, small and then larger, accompany your welcome of truthful ideas.

694. With a cosmic conscience we see that anything done against others is also done against ourselves.

695. Everyone yearns to live his own life, but how many will change his thinking to attain it?

696. Be on guard against destructive attitudes which insist they have come to protect you.

697. There is a part within every human being in which time is absent, in which hours and days and years have no meaning.

698. Imaginary happiness must be kept in place by tense struggles, while real happiness stays in place all by itself.

699. Anyone who has forgotten who he is and what he should be doing can take right inner action to remember.

700. As you study and act, remember that the whole idea is to reveal yourself to yourself.

8

How to Attract
Higher Help Quickly

In the days of sailing ships a vessel left
Tahiti with the intended destination of San
Francisco. A sudden storm wrecked the ship
and left the crew on a deserted island. The sea-
men had but one way to attract help. Hiking to
the nearest crest, they prepared a bonfire. On
the fifth night a passing ship sighted the fire
and rescued the sailors.

A sincere request for life-rescue is an
accurate and an intelligent action. It will be

answered by a higher power whose purpose is rescue.

The bonfire was not prepared or lighted by the rescuing ship. This was the task of the stranded sailors. By doing their part they established contact with what they needed. *Contact.* That is the magic word. Any earnest man or woman can start making contact with higher help by developing right thoughts. One right thought is a willingness to abandon familiar and fixed beliefs. Changing ourselves instead of trying to change the world is another.

Perhaps you see a fascinating feature in all this. You are really trying to make contact with yourself, with who you really are. Call it the kingdom of heaven within, call it your real self, call it cosmic consciousness, it is the same certain deliverance.

The teachings of this chapter will help you make permanent contact with your own rescue ship.

How to Attract Higher Help Quickly

701. The point is to change your relationship with yourself and with the world by changing your relationship with Truth.

702. The power that attracts higher answers is the admission of not presently having them.

703. If you want the truly inspirational you need only seek out the truly factual.

704. The seeker finally finds when his habitual values yield to something much higher.

705. It is not your part to create the new world but to permit it to reveal itself.

706. As long as the usual nature judges between right and wrong it will be wrong.

707. Your recovered essence easily makes right decisions because it has no false self to protect.

708. Intelligence consists of using all the available aids for escape, such as seeing the need for it.

709. Truth gazes down upon wandering humanity and thinks, "If only they would pause long enough to *listen.*"

710. Turning to God, Truth, Reality, simply means to let go, even fearfully at first, of our self-centered ideas.

711. A new kind of mind comes into existence by seeing clearly the limitations of the usual mind.

712. The best time to permit higher facts to help you is when you cannot see how they can do so.

713. A sincere wish for help activates fresh intelligence for finding higher help.

714. Truth never speaks to surface personality but only to the interior essence of a man or woman.

715. Stop telling yourself who you are, for then a higher voice will make everything clear.

716. Descending into unknown regions in yourself is the same as making the upward journey.

717. An earnest attempt to understand higher facts is a success in itself, regardless of the results of the attempt.

718. The individual who *really* wants to give himself over to higher guidance will receive it.

719. You are accepted by truth the same moment you accept truth, even in a small way at first.

720. Whether aware of it or not you have a permanent invitation from truth, so be aware of it.

How Self-Newness Arrives

721. Self-newness comes by turning back to the

cosmic home within, and turning back a dozen times a day.

722. If you cannot take it any more, now is the time to turn toward higher powers which can take anything.

723. Anyone who has placed himself beyond the reach of higher help can start today to place himself within reach.

724. The ability to follow major instructions is developed by devotion to small instructions.

725. Devote yourself to the instruction, "Let a love of rightness succeed where your usual efforts fail."

726. Regardless of how you presently feel about it, there is an available answer to every baffling question.

727. You can rise to a higher level of consciousness by seeing how the lower level hurts you.

728. Real solutions are discovered only where they actually exist–within the individual's own essence.

729. Acquire spiritual knowledge and then use it to go on to the supreme act of self-transcendence.

730. Life-giving sincerity consists of an earnest

attempt to hear something higher than ourselves.

731. Heavenly guidance for earthly affairs is quite possible, providing we live from the kingdom of heaven within.

732. If sensing a real source of help, within or without, let nothing stop you from reaching it.

733. There is a level of teaching much higher than words heard only by those who know more than words.

734. Take a new internal direction and it will be as real to you as traveling down a new highway.

735. Keep the inner task clear and simple by remembering, "There is something wrong which I can correct."

736. Truth waits patiently for us to see that we must approach on its terms, not our own.

737. Let feelings of helplessness fall on a wish for higher strength, not on despair.

738. By reading this book you are impressing yourself with the fact of a greater good for yourself.

739. To qualify for the cosmic college we need only realize how little we know about life.

740. One thing that truth appreciates from you is your enthusiasm in seeking it out.

Hear Celestial Inspirations

741. A willingness to learn will develop our talent for hearing celestial inspirations when they try to reach us.

742. The presence of an enlightened person can remind you that the Answer exists, but go from reminding to possession.

743. If you feel that real and practical wisdom is too high for you, just remember that real wisdom is a permanent feature of your true inner nature.

744. Self-wholeness is won by no longer following the ideas that have produced a lack of it.

745. Never worriedly ask what will replace wrong ideas, but know that the replacement will always be right for you.

746. Permit the powers of your essence to break down the walls of separation and they will do so.

747. To know nothing but the invented self is to know nothing but sadness, so turn toward the celestial self.

748. Only one power can break the repetitious circle of one's life–and you are now studying that unique power.

749. Simply realize that you can stand aside and observe your thoughts instead of being carried away by them.

750. Give yourself permission to receive your real benefits and you will receive them.

751. Coming to an end of yourself means to realize the folly of using old ideas to create a new nature.

752. The moment you stop fighting to retain your habitual notions is the same moment you feel higher help.

753. The power that called you to these lofty lessons will also help you understand them.

754. Admit your inability to take care of yourself, for that invites Reality to take care of you *in its right way.*

755. Only the higher part of you has an interest in and has a response to cosmic teachings.

756. Help is available whether we are aware of it or not, but awareness makes it active.

757. Right ideas connect you with higher help, and more right ideas strengthen that connection.

758. We need only look at our negative states and ask, "Can these have anything good for me?"

759. It is easy to declare that one wants help, but quite another matter to really welcome it.

760. A crisis is used rightly when it turns you toward self-examination and self-insight.

Your Secret Book

761. There is within you a secret book that knows a thousand times more than all the scholars and authorities on earth.

762. Sincerely desire to search and the instrument for a right search will be supplied.

763. Truth is seen with the development of spiritual eyesight, which is not the same as ordinary thinking.

764. Seeing that the problem is really within oneself is a healthy drink of the healing medicine.

765. Cosmic hearing consists of the ability to hear and follow the teachings of your own higher centers.

766. We must see that the pressures of life are caused by personal misunderstanding, which . the welcomed light can correct.

767. Truth alone can heal the life, but the individual alone must ask for it.

768. Life is solved by seeing it without self-reference, which is the celestial view.

769. An awareness of neglect of spiritual necessities is a power in itself for attracting those necessities.

770. We are lonely only because of absence from our cosmic home, so what is the sure cure for loneliness?

771. Let the higher part call the lower part back from its wandering in the wilderness.

772. Authentic knowledge of yourself and knowledge of God, Truth, Reality, are the same thing.

773. Your essence can be sensible for you when you cannot be sensible for yourself, so join your essence.

774. There are sincere and there are insincere cries for help, and knowing the difference, truth responds to only one of them.

775. A proper prayer is simply the gallant wish to unite with who you really are.

776. Truth is the only power capable of correcting us ten thousand times without rejecting us once.

777. Open even one small window of your psychic home and you will feel the result in cosmic sunshine.

778. When asking, "Where am I thinking wrongly about this problem?" You should answer, "By trying to use ordinary thought for a success possible only for cosmic consciousness."

779. Remember that the sighting of a new weakness must precede the acquisition of a new strength.

780. True guidance comes to those who have lost confidence in their usual mental maps.

Know Who You Really Are

781. Let the truth shake up your identity as much as it wishes, for it wants only to show you who you really are.

782. You are really one note in the Cosmic Music, harmonizing with other notes to form a grand symphony.

783. Anyone can save himself by ceasing to believe that stubborn self-will is protective self-loyalty.

784. A persistent refusal to believe in your own captivity will release you.

785. A silent glance from a real teacher helps a student, for the student senses the teacher's commanding rightness.

786. Proceed from the human view to cosmic vision and the obscure will become clear.

787. Forcefully decline to go along with wrong ways and the right ways will reveal themselves.

788. There is a part in everyone which is not his usual nature, and by this he is saved.

789. The inner instructor is always trying to be heard above our noisy minds, so give it a chance.

790. An innocent spirit on the path flies easily over the walls that block an insincere spirit.

791. Anyone who is his own punishment does not realize it, so awareness can be his great escape.

792. Be willing to accept what is true and in time you will know what is true.

793. It is possible to turn a problem over to God providing you do not secretly demand *your* solution.

794. When realizing that repetitious thought cannot help us we are coming closer to real help.

795. The needed light will shine at the exact moment that we stop pretending we already live in it.

796. Do it because it is right, not for the reward, for then the reward will be real.

797. Rightness rushes in to fill the space made possible by first giving up wrongness.

798. The higher lesson in the experience is learned by those who no longer protect their vanity.

799. A right response to a higher truth is to relax and let it tell its whole story.

800. Choose to understand, stick with that choice, and the whole world of truth takes your side.

9

Why the Human Jungle
is Dangerous

Some students of the inner life asked their instructor, "Why does human chaos continue in spite of all efforts at correction?" Replied the teacher, "Trying to solve human problems with the same kind of mind that causes them is like asking a destructive tornado to rebuild the town it has just destroyed."

The mind capable of curing the human condition is the mind that has risen above its own wrong ideas.

Why the Human Jungle is Dangerous

How many human beings have risen above their cherished but wrong ideas? How many have even made the slightest effort to do so? Not many. Astonishingly, most people fight fiercely to defend their false notions–the very notions that cause their conflict and misery! It is like an ill man who locks the door when seeing the doctor approach with the healing medicine.

That is why the human jungle is dangerous.

And that is why you must aim to not live like most people.

Where they fight facts, you can welcome them. Where they wish to be impressive, you can wish to be real. Where they cling to self-defeating opinions, you can seek self-enlightening principles. Where they prefer bitterness over the past, you can choose liberty in the now.

Let this chapter explain clearly why you should not live like most people. Then you will not cry like most people.

Why the Human Jungle
is Dangerous

801. The world consists of imaginary people claiming imaginary virtues and suffering from imaginary happiness.

802. Anyone attributing nonexistent virtues to himself will also attribute them to others, which explains human heartache.

803. A man plants weeds instead of flowers because his vanity assumes it knows the difference in the two.

804. All talk about uplifting human conditions without uplifting human nature is pure delusion.

805. People who love the human jungle will make every effort to prevent your escape from it.

806. Because man lives in imagination he imagines the nature of God, Truth, Reality–and misses the mark.

807. A jungle-mind scoffs at the idea that there is another land beyond the jungle.

808. What a hypocritical society calls concern for other people is simply an obsessive attempt to make a lie appear as a fact.

809. Humanity walks in its sleep, with everyone

trying to convince himself and others that he is awake.

810. What happens to a ship when the captain dozes at the wheel while *dreaming* he is in command?

811. A sure sign that one is living in a state of psychic sleep is his disinterest or disbelief or scorn when told that this is his state.

812. Everyone who is allergic to reality wastes his life trying to prove he is not allergic.

813. For every sane person who sees the folly of fighting there are ten million people who claim to see it.

814. A man can obtain something he insists is valuable, but then he has to find a way to get rid of it.

815. Feeling persecuted is very valuable to those who want to remain in the darkness of egotism.

816. Because their natures are so utterly different, an eagle never consents to talking with a parrot.

817. The chief trouble with a parrot is his arrogant insistence that he is an eagle.

818. Refusal to face the unpleasant facts about human nature is a form of self-betrayal.

819. Only a defeated person is ready for rescue, but unfortunately many people like to claim defeat without meaning it.

820. Healing fails to occur simply because it is much easier to injure others than to heal oneself.

A Strange Fact

821. How strange that people pretend to know themselves when it is possible to really know.

822. Truly intelligent behavior cannot be explained to nor understood by the unintelligent.

823. You can recognize a false teaching by the way it permits its followers to talk like angels while behaving like demons.

824. Darkness plays it safe by never venturing close to a light which would expose it as darkness.

825. Everyone thinks he is different, but the truly different person is one not living in unconscious conceit.

826. One evil becomes the victim of another evil because both evils masquerade as the good.

827. People living in imaginary goodness never

see the great danger they are to themselves.

828. When your inner being dwells above the hostile forces in the world, the hostile forces do not exist for you.

829. Unreceptive humans cannot hear the message of cosmic health any more than a fish can hear music.

830. Ponder deeply the fact that a spiritually ignorant man does not know that he does not know.

831. Falsehood and vanity are uncomfortable at a meeting where truth is really taught.

832. Do you think a person who has really found God, Truth, and Reality, would have concealed contempt for other people?

833. Being a danger to oneself and a danger to others are the same danger.

834. People in danger from themselves reveal it when angrily hearing of the good fortune of enemies.

835. Anyone can conceal anger, but the spiritual hero is one who ends its cause, which is unconscious egotism.

836. Love of truth and involvement with religious activities are two totally different things.

837. Every action arising from darkness which calls itself light can only deepen the darkness.

838. We carelessly talked ourselves into the jungle but can now wisely plan our way out of it.

839. By seeing that a problem exists only in misunderstanding, we wisely refrain from causing a problem.

840. People think they are acting from love and service when they are really acting from guilt and showmanship.

The Entire Explanation

841. Self-deceived men deceive other self-deceived men, and that explains entirely the dreadful human condition.

842. Nothing of true value is won when it is won through the pressures of human organization.

843. Neurosis has a thousand lying explanations, but never really knows why it does anything.

844. What is seen as right and normal by society is seen as immature distortion by a free mind.

845. Stubborn man insists that the shadow is sunshine, then complains at the lack of warmth!

846. A hardened man could hear the greatest teacher of the ages and walk away still hardened.

847. Your right nature has total power over every wrong man or woman on earth.

848. Human evil is a result of psychic hypnosis, which cosmic consciousness can cure.

849. A false teacher is the uncomfortable and resentful slave of those he teaches.

850. Humanity is like someone who sends complimentary letters to himself, pretending they are real.

851. The individual can be artificial in public or he can be real in private but he cannot be both.

852. Heaven sighs when human beings make a list of moral standards they intend to follow.

853. Wrongness is incapable of recognizing rightness because it wrongly calls itself right.

854. The perfect way to never see that one is his own great enemy is to constantly accuse others.

855. An awakened man knows what will happen to an unawakened man, but also knows the unpopularity of his vital message.

856. One sign of an immature mind is the ease

and frequency with which it feels offended.

857. It is easy for public reformers to feel sorry for the world with other people's money.

858. Is anything more foolish than to refuse the light and then complain about falling in the dark?

859. Falsehood believes it is talking with truth, when it is only muttering to itself.

860. What is praised as sticking to one's principles is usually only a stubborn refusal to learn something new.

Sheep and Wolf

861. A sheep invites a wolf into the meadow because the sheep stupidly believes the wolf's smile is real.

862. Man's incredible contradiction is his wish to change himself without changing himself.

863. The less a man governs himself the more he feels qualified to govern others.

864. A person who enjoys his conflicts will not be interested in the explanation for ending them.

865. A petty mind finds it easy to deceive other petty minds, after which it returns to its own misery.

866. The world is not ruled by human beings or

by laws but by outer appearances.

867. A person who departs from a real teacher never realizes the damage he has done to himself.

868. Egotism is fearfully alert in detecting danger to itself, and flees at the first appearance of decency.

869. Anyone who cannot be told what he actually is cannot be told what he can actually become.

870. The person who pays the price for self-deception is the person who practices self-deception.

871. The vibration of vanity is taken as happiness by those lost in unhappiness.

872. Destructive vanity can be ended by doing precisely what vanity does not want us to do, for example, by admitting a present lack of comprehension of life.

873. A surface admission of confusion about life is not enough, for that can be vanity's trick to avoid facing a deep confusion.

874. Ignorance is simply a lack of knowledge, while stupidity is a refusal to collect needed knowledge.

875. Do not believe it when neurotic indignation tries to pass itself off as righteousness.

876. One tragedy of being inwardly asleep is that an awakened man does not exist to our perception, therefore his aid is ignored.

877. Negative thinking causes self-agitation, but cosmic consciousness supplies self-contentment.

878. A conditioned mind can teach right living about as much as a small child can teach astronomy.

879. Insincere seeking finds what it wants to find, while sincere seeking finds what jolts but cures.

880. False teachings strive to appear mysterious, for they really know that most people prefer mysteries to solutions.

Give No False Rewards

881. Stop giving bothersome people false rewards and they will stop bothering you.

882. It is wrong to reward weak people out of a sense of guilt, for that only encourages their weakness.

883. You find people unattractive because you

sense that their displayed strength is artificial.

884. In spite of an exterior show of confidence, anyone with an artificial light always fears it will fail, spilling him into the pit.

885. The real solution to social problems cannot be explained to anyone who does not want to hear *himself ex*plained.

886. It is wrong for you to enter into a human relationship on the demanding terms of another person.

887. When habitual thought supplies an answer to a problem, that answer becomes the next problem.

888. You are truly loved by someone who does not accept your wrong behavior as right, and that is very rare.

889. Never accept the confused or unpleasant behavior of other people as your problem, for it is theirs alone.

890. Ignorance is unable to see danger because it flatters itself with the label of intelligence.

891. Is the truly intelligent person the one who fights the truth or the one who uses it?

892. Human sickness is so severe that few can bear to look at it, but those who do will become well.

893. A neurotic fish looked up at a soaring bird and sighed, "Poor creature who does not know the fun of muddy water."

894. It is useless and wrong to try to help people who want your attention but not your help.

895. Right answers can be found only in a right source, and human creeds are not that source.

896. Just as you examine a purchase for its quality, examine ideas offered you for value to your real nature.

897. Truth does not exist to be organized and interpreted by man, but to save him.

898. It rarely occurs to people that they can solve the problem by solving themselves.

899. The human jungle is not dangerous to those whose insight has carried them out of it.

900. The whole secret for escaping the human jungle is to work inwardly, rightly, persistently.

10

Let Your Mind Work with Full Power

In a science class the young pupils took turns at finding distant objects through a telescope. One boy peered and remarked, "But I can't see my home." The teacher handed him a larger telescope with the comment, "You need a superior viewpoint."

And so do we. It is the cosmic viewpoint which sees life wholly and understands it thoroughly. That peaceful viewpoint is obtainable.

No one would dream of neglecting the

natural powers of the sun, of rivers and winds, of seeds and gravity. Yet how few people ever really reflect upon the natural powers of the mind–powers which can be individually acquired, controlled, and used for superior daily actions. Why this neglect?

Well, many men and women believe the human mind is much too mysterious to enter and explore. Not at all. It is a happy fact that the mind can learn to understand the mind. It can be compared with entering a castle, one room at a time, observing and comprehending how each room contributes its part to the orderly function of the castle as a whole. Take the power of habit. We know how some habits work against us, as when frequently falling into worry. But habit can also be a positive force, as when we faithfully study the mind.

As you now study other specific mental powers, remember the declaration of Ralph Waldo Emerson: "Nothing is at last sacred but the integrity of your own mind."

Let Your Mind Work
with Full Power

901. To state it as simply as possible, you can use your mind in a totally different way, a way having no strife or regret, a way as natural as the flow of a peaceful river.

902. Let your personal mind go right and your personal world goes right effortlessly.

903. Never let the mind of any other person tell you that it is superior to your mind.

904. Deliberately slow down your inner world of thoughts and feelings, then be ready for some astonishing discoveries.

905. Realize that old mental habits can only repeat the same unhappy results, for that awakens fresh power for self-newness.

906. Remind yourself constantly that the false wisdom of society can only make everything worse.

907. Turn away from society's artificial wisdom to the real intelligence of your recovered essence.

908. The mind can be a wall or an open gate before Reality, depending upon which one we make it.

909. A sudden situation may require your thought, but it never requires your distress.

910. What your ordinary mind cannot understand can be grasped fully by your developing higher mind.

911. What you can become is far greater than you think, so with delight rise above habitual thinking.

912. The only way to feel in a new and superior way is to let the cosmic college teach you to think in a new way.

913. It is harmful error to assume we understand something simply because it agrees with what we already believe.

914. Wanting rescuing ideas while clinging to personal beliefs is like trying to add new items to a packed closet.

915. It is valuable to see how negative thoughts cause negative actions which cause negative feelings.

916. We are under the harmful power of any wrong idea we refuse to see as wrong.

917. We are under the healthy power of any right idea we admit to replace a wrong idea.

918. Learn to think in short and clear sentences

which summarize good and guiding ideas.

919. An example of a clear sentence is "Nothing is more essential than to discover the truth about life for myself."

920. Deliberately interrupt your thoughts during the day to ponder an idea of special interest to you.

The Power of Real Intelligence

921. Real intelligence, cosmic intelligence, quietly knows itself, having no compulsion to promote or protect itself.

922. What beautiful freedom in not having to strain at proving how intelligent we are!

923. Consider wrong thoughts as unnecessary distractions to pleasant days.

924. One sign of immature minds is their incapacity to learn the lessons in personal or historical disasters.

925. It is possible to sense the existence of higher ways, which supplies incentive for obtainment.

926. How strange that a person will carefully attend to his home or his finances, yet will completely neglect the development of his own mind.

927. Real happiness is the natural result of having a cosmically mature mind.

928. Contacting pure Truth and contacting our *personal ideas about Truth* are two different and opposite actions.

929. A personal idea about Truth is not Truth itself any more than an idea about a mountain is an actual mountain.

930. The alternative to human wretchedness is found by abandoning habitual thinking.

931. Habitual thinking is ended by ceasing to promote and protect the illusion of having a separate self.

932. We do not wish other people to interfere with us, so why permit harmful thoughts to interfere?

933. A man who merely thinks that he thinks for himself must pay the high price for his error.

934. A truly mature mind can be neither hurt nor flattered, for its very maturity is its independent stability.

935. Cosmic clarity is as different from ordinary thought as the sea is different from the desert.

936. Many claim to have gone beyond their usual thinking channels, but only the free have done so.

937. Deliberately break away from vagabond thoughts which try to lead you into dark places.

938. We must simply see that the present way we think is not the only way to think.

939. One sign of mental maturity is to comprehend the power and delight of simplicity.

940. The fuel of wrong action is wrong thinking, while the fuel of right action is cosmic consciousness.

What You Can Do for Yourself

941. Attend to what you can do for yourself, not on what you think others can do against you.

942. A good reason for removing errors of thinking is that we will cease to suffer from them.

943. Foolish minds hope to benefit exterior personality, while wise minds wish to enrich inner essence.

944. The deeper part of your mind, which appears with your invitation, wants something unlike the surface part.

945. How rarely it occurs to anyone to use his mind in a new way to make his life a better life.

946. Something higher than the ordinary mind can teach it to function correctly, and that higher power is God, Truth, Reality.

947. Lack of psychic sunshine indicates we have not really opened the mental window.

948. A mind eager for inner discovery may be temprorily baffled but will never be disappointed.

949. Inquire whether your thinking is true, healthy, necessary, sincere, pleasant.

950. Anyone complaining he was led astray by others is admitting he has no mind of his own.

951. A man who would not eat unhealthy foods not only consumes but welcomes unhealthy thoughts.

952. A mind living in a prison of its own making has the ability to become its own key to liberty.

953. One day you will see delightfully that you are no longer thinking in your usual ways.

954. Most people with confused minds can neither see nor admit it, which is why their self-haunting continues.

955. A sleeping man lives on the intellectual level

only, while an awakened man lives above it.

956. Cosmic comprehension and intellectual cleverness are as far apart as head and heel.

957. Useless and tiring thinking falls away as you advance with these teachings.

958. Like replacing a wrong book with the right one, learn to read your real self, not adopted ideas.

959. Open the door to your real nature by learning what it means to drop mechanical thoughts.

960. The difference between right and wrong is known only by cosmic consciousness, not by the ordinary mind.

A Flash of Insight

961. One flash of cosmic insight can solve a thousand problems caused by the habitual mind.

962. If you wonder why your life is what it is, notice how your mind works.

963. Remember that a really new life must be created with new thoughts, so see what it means to think freshly.

964. Problems are not solved by fighting them, but by lifting the mind above the level of combat.

965. Can truth penetrate a mind which unconsciously twists it to fit its own self-centered beliefs?

966. Repeated thoughts create the illusion of a troubled self, so replace wrong thoughts with perception.

967. A cosmic castle cannot be built with dark thoughts any more than a home can be built with shadows.

968. Think about inner conflict, then think how quietness would make everything different.

969. You can have something different if persistently willing to think something different.

970. How astonishing that people believe that a confused mind can create clear conditions.

971. It is possible to hear something quite different by ceasing to love the noise of our own minds.

972. Never fear to see what you are really thinking, for that leads to self-liberation.

973. In spite of all appearances we are chained only by our own lack of clear comprehension.

974. You are using these principles in order to *think about yourself in a new way.*

975. As a healthy mental exercise simply

ponder what it means to think in a totally new way.

976. Let ordinary thinking come to an end, and extraordinary thinking will begin.

977. Answers from the conditioned mind will always be wrong, though appearing right, while answers from purified essence will always be right, though at first appearing wrong.

978. A new mind is possible to attain, providing you are quite dissatisfied with your old mind.

979. If you hesitate to empty your mind of its present contents, just detect the harm in its contents.

980. Just as a mountaineer sees the world differently than a farmer, so does a higher mind have a unique view of humanity.

Let Your Mind Serve You

981. Insight into your mind changes thoughts from noisy dictators into quiet servants.

982. Notice how tension and anger arise in an exposed person, which proves that hidden thoughts cause pain.

983. Hidden thoughts and wrong thoughts are handled intelligently and cured only by awareness of them.

984. The more intelligent the mind the more it deliberately questions its present positions.

985. See that your mental picture of yourself is not your real self and troubles fall away.

986. The intelligent reaction toward trouble is to ask, "How can I think clearly toward this?"

987. To think clearly is to think without references to the past, without false ideas about ourselves.

988. This is a science of freedom in which you learn to not go along with enslaving thoughts and emotions.

989. The rescuing facts are not what we assume they are, which is why they can succeed where our assumptions cannot.

990. Just let the thought occur to you that there is another way to live, for that is a true and powerful thought.

991. Profitable effort consists of a patient attempt to make a small idea clear to your mind.

992. Remember that a thought about yourself is a thought only, not the true and whole you.

993. Society wants to take over your mind, and can you think of anything more disastrous?

994. We must proceed from ordinary thought to

cosmic insight, for merely thinking about the Celestial City does not place us in it any more than thinking about a star places us on it.

995. The mind rightly turns to both inward and outward things, but you are made new by the inward look.

996. Wrong conditions are corrected by having right attitudes toward them.

997. Higher truths have great power to dissolve mental mists, making your life clear to you.

998. When the mind is truly quiet, its statements and answers are truly accurate.

999. Ordinary thought cannot solve personal or social problems because it is the very cause of those problems.

1000. There is a completely new way to travel through life, and you are now on that wondrous way.

11

Learn to Live Your Own Free Life

A prisoner-of-war pondered the reason for his gloom and frustration. He saw that the reason was simple enough. The confinement prevented him from living his own life. Urged on by his dissatisfaction, he planned his escape, which succeeded.

A feeling that one is not living a life of his own is a good and essential step toward living one's own life. Like that prisoner-of-war, our realization of self-imprisonment is intelligence in itself for making our escape.

Learn to Live Your Own Free Life

Stated differently, seeing our sorrows and confusions can lead to a dynamic decision–the decision to seek the way out of ourselves. Author Leo Tolstoy describes this valorous decision: "There comes a time, when, on the one hand a vague awakening consciousness stirs the soul, the consciousness of the higher law . . . and the sufferings a man endures from the contradictions of life, compel him to renounce the social order and to adopt the new . . . And this time has now arrived."

What Tolstoy calls an "awakening consciousness" is a truly marvelous experience, open to all who welcome it. It is a well-known stage to everyone who has ever escaped the human jungle.

Where others have succeeded, you can succeed. No one is denied. Allow the following instructions to awaken your consciousness. Let them lead you to the liberty known and enjoyed by others.

Learn to Live Your Own Free Life

1001. What you really want is a life that is truly your own, which is what these teachings are all about.

1002. Do not feel guilty about wanting a life of your own, for your own real life is a totally unselfish life.

1003. Discover what it means to live your own life, and as a clue it means to not accept society's values.

1004. Seek cosmic strength, for there is no way for human weakness to touch the truly strong individual.

1005. Permit no glittering attraction to lure you away from your supreme aim of self-knowledge.

1006. Let others tell you what is right and you suffer from their being wrong, though you may not see it.

1007. Let your essence tell you what is right and you will be right, and you will know it.

1008. You conquer the world by understanding it, and this idea is a thousand times deeper than it appears.

1009. When people criticize you, they merely

mean that you are not conforming to their particular nonsense.

1010. Imaginary duties and imaginary virtues never let us rest, so detect and dismiss them.

1011. Become aware that you are not now leading yourself through life, and you can learn to lead.

1012. The true artist is the one who has mastered the art of living in quiet competence with himself.

1013. Let these ideas show you what you really want and what you do not want.

1014. Be the one person in a thousand who gives earnest thought as to why he is here on earth.

1015. If scared over the decision to choose the real life, just choose it and fear will vanish.

1016. Stand up for yourself in the right way, which means to stand inside your own cosmic nature.

1017. Pay no attention when a weak world insists you must be part of its weakness.

1018. A person can have the temporary approval of his friends or he can have his own life, but he cannot have both.

1019. To know that you must start inner change is already an excellent start.

1020. A positive experience is a negative experience handled consciously.

Understand Human Nature

1021. Seek facts about human nature, for you are at the mercy of every man or woman you fail to understand.

1022. Truth knows it is true, so when you become truth you will have no more doubts about yourself.

1023. Be loyal to who you really are, and all questions about loyalty to others will be answered.

1024. Increase your inner wealth by increasing your wish to live your own life.

1025. The reason you can draw new wisdom from yourself is because it exists in the new areas being uncovered.

1026. Never permit the shallow lives of others to injure the profound life you must find.

1027. Since society is capable of producing only bad news, why not turn to the good news of your own essence?

1028. New ways appear just as swiftly as our realization that the old ways cannot do anything right.

1029. A tremendous secret is contained in the words, "Be your own world."

1030. It is up to us to understand truth, and not our task to try to make truth understand us.

1031. Your internal scenery can remain fresh and green, regardless of a dry external world.

1032. Distress indicates a lack of mental clearness, and since clearness is possible, distress is unnecessary.

1033. Notice how people try to make you think about things you really want to ignore, then ignore.

1034. Release and relief from internal chains are what these teachings are all about.

1035. Practice all day long at dropping negative impressions the moment they try to enter.

1036. The psychic enemy is personal negativity, which is conquered by self-knowledge.

1037. The true king of himself has no need whatever to have bowing subjects.

1038. Obey your own higher nature and you will never need to obey the lower nature of another person.

1039. Develop the part of you which never consents to being intimidated by other people.
1040. Know that you need not please anyone or anything but your own real nature.

React for Your Own Richness

1041. Forget the right reaction for society and find the right reaction for *you*.
1042. Suspect that you may be responding from society instead of from yourself and you will begin to respond rightly.
1043. Few people see that deliverance means self-deliverance, but those who see it will deliver themselves.
1044. We cease to stray from truth when finally realizing that truth is our very own and very wealthy original nature.
1045. Try to see that the room you now occupy is not the entire cosmic castle.
1046. One of the great cosmic medicines of the ages is, "See yourself as you really are."
1047. You can spend all day in self-discovery, whether in field or factory or home.
1048. If you want strong leadership, be your

own leader, for this is a power of your real nature.

1049. The majority is wrong and the minority is wrong, for only cosmic truth is right.

1050. Relying on guidance from the outside is like trusting a tornado to carry you home.

1051. Everyone senses that the only person who can be strong for him is himself, and that clue is worth following.

1052. Your own rich resources will show you where to look, what to do, and how to do it.

1053. You may be presently captured by a negative feeling, but you are not its permanent slave.

1054. Do what is unpopular with your usual nature and you will do what is right for your new nature.

1055. A chief duty of yours is to ignore the duties that other people insist you owe them.

1056. It may appear unkind to leave people with their own responsibilities, but it is a truly helpful act, for they can grow no other way.

1057. Seeing the folly of merely changing exterior locations can start refreshing inner change.

1058. There is no way to hurt the feelings of someone living with his true identity, with his cosmic self.

1059. The only proof of rightness is the rightness of your own real nature which never needs to consult human opinion.

1060. Your own released light will guide you safely and accurately along your own trail.

Conquer the World
in a New Way

1061. Conquer your inner world and you will see clearly that it was the only necessary conquest.

1062. At a certain point in your progress you will see what it means to be your own teacher.

1063. When finally learning what it means to treat ourselves rightly, we have no concern over our treatment by others.

1064. The one way to live another life is to let these principles make you another person.

1065. Be attentive always to your own rightness, never being distracted by the wrongness of others.

1066. Remember that society's dangerous nonsense always disguises itself as something profound and necessary.

1067. Be like a tree so filled with nature's wisdom that it cares for its own growth, never interfering with other trees.

1068. One day you will see that the right part of you was right after all.

1069. The turning point can occur by seeing that we can deceive others but never really deceive ourselves.

1070. You have your own life to lead, and that life is free from trembling before other people.

1071. You are not responsible for anyone who stubbornly chooses to ruin his own life.

1072. One way to remain a self-prisoner is to complain, "How come they get away with things I cannot?"

1073. We must first see what we are really like, for that awareness is power for becoming who we really are.

1074. Can you think of anything more dreadful than to be tyrannized by the unreal parts of us which we fail to see?

1075. If you want a plan having a totally new

kind of reward, plan to find your natural self.

1076. You can discover who you really are by bravely declining to be who you usually are.

1077. Learning to live your own life includes learning to say no to the neurotic demands of others.

1078. Never agree with the choice of millions of human beings who have chosen darkness while calling it light.

1079. The great goal is to understand life *from yourself,* not from what others have told you.

1080. You can have the opinions of your friends or you can have the liberating facts, but you cannot have both.

Build Your Cosmic Castle

1081. A teacher's work is to supply you with right construction materials with which you can build your own cosmic castle.

1082. Have no hesitation in seeing the trivial as trivial, for that invites the truly important.

1083. The only thing that maintains a wall between you and real riches is your belief in a wall.

1084. Never sacrifice a feeling of what is right in order to please wrong people.

1085. When spiritual facts are not accompanied by the erasing of egotism, we fall into imaginary spirituality.

1086. We gain what is truly our own by dropping wrong notions of what is our own.

1087. Quietly refuse to be intimidated by anyone who tries to threaten you in any way.

1088. Any voice that criticizes your wish to find your real nature is a false voice you should ignore.

1089. The louder the old nature objects to its dismissal the faster it should be dismissed.

1090. Rightness resting in truth banishes anxiety over being right in the eyes of other people.

1091. Ignorance of self places us under negative influences, which are lifted only by self-insight.

1092. Observe the stumbling in other people as lessons for ending the stumbling in yourself.

1093. Stop the interference of wrong thoughts and watch your day unfold smoothly and directly.

1094. How delightful to realize that one need no longer be a burden to himself!

1095. Just as you might disconnect a noisy motor, right thinking disconnects you from the world's woes.

1096. Friends and fortunes may leave you, but it makes no difference to your new nature.

1097. The laws of your own original nature are perfect, having no strains nor contradictions.

1098. Release the right part of you and it will instantly know right from wrong actions.

1099. Love what you are doing for your inner self and watch how true riches accumulate.

1100. Each time you treasure these ideas you reclaim a part of your own life.

12

Secret Plans for Escaping the Jungle

A traveler wanted to reach a distant country. His friends gave him dozens of maps, assuring him of their accuracy. But the maps turned out to be faulty after all, so the traveler wasted considerable time and energy in confused wandering. He finally realized what had to be done. Tossing the maps aside he exclaimed, "Thank heaven, I now know a wrong road when I see one. Now I can find the right road for myself." No doubt you have often felt the same way about it. You probably sense the necessity for breaking away from everything you have been told about life in order to rely upon your own mental lamps. That is both a bold and a sensible feeling! You will always go right by following it. You will always go right because you will be following nothing but your own released essence, your own liberated light.

Make an experiment as you cover the one hundred points of this chapter. It consists simply of being aware of something. Be aware of how truth believes in you, has cheerful confidence in you, knows about your ability to win higher success. Falsehood can never do this, for it has no confidence in itself or in anything else. But truth can and does see you as finally victorious. So just see how aware you can be that truth is on your side. Now, what more could you want than that!

Secret Plans for Escaping the Jungle

1101. A simple wish to start fresh has power to cancel past mistakes and let you begin anew.

1102. Right submission is to submit to what is right within yourself, so seek this rightness.

1103. The true strength of an awakened man can be felt and appreciated only by those who are beginning to awaken.

1104. Hopelessness can either pretend it is not hopeless or it can start to fade through use of these ideas.

1105. Our happy task is to be unlimited in the amount of help we can take from the limitless Source.

1106. Something much higher than calculating our way through life is to have inner command of life.

1107. The unfamiliar is not an enemy to be feared, as many believe, but the door to freedom from fear.

1108. Develop a new kind of intensity, one that wants to go up, not against.

1109. Never forget that the vast majority of

human beings have no interest at all in inner awakening.

1110. The success of a real spiritual group is measured by the number of people who do not come back.

1111. That rare person who really sees his betrayal by his own wrong ideas is ready to awaken.

1112. Yield to the part of you that sees the futility of clinging fearfully to incorrectness.

1113. Just as cunning aids a fox in escaping his pursuers, these lessons aid your escape from troubles.

1114. Real courage and humility are expressed in, "Maybe I have been all wrong up to now."

1115. It is needful to see that something is wrong, but not needful to condemn yourself for wrongness.

1116. Imagination insists it is reality, and you must emphatically insist it is not.

1117. When with human beings remember that only a small part of their motives are visible.

1118. When having the courage to stop crying, "What am I going to do?" We will know exactly what to do.

Secret Plans for Escaping the Jungle

1119. The only thing that really prevents us from being right is the false fear of being wrong.

1120. To think with a whole mind we must first see our captivity by divided thoughts.

Invite Fresh Health

1121. When first seeing our need to escape the jungle we feel a strange anxiety, but this passes, leaving us with fresh health.

1122. We seek truth rightly by recognizing and eliminating falsehood of every kind.

1123. We can always recognize human artificiality by its angry fear of getting exposed.

1124. Take shocks as signs of being in psychic sleep, then use them for self-awakening.

1125. Absorb the fact that you are not who you imagine you are and it will carry you all the way out of the jungle.

1126. Wishing to see higher facts without effort is like wanting to travel without movement.

1127. Resolve today to go all out in breaking down and traveling beyond the inner wall.

1128. Write down and remember helpful words, such as quietness, study, receptivity, alertness, simplicity.

1129. Truth declares that a new you is possible, so why hesitate in the inner quest?

1130. The assumption that you are doing the best you can do prevents you from doing much better.

1131. An awakened person is not hoaxed by evil as are others, which is why he alone can help others.

1132. The sternness of man is fear masquerading as strength, while the sternness of truth is love.

1133. A wise seeker asks, "If my own way is so right how come I feel so wrong?"

1134. For good or bad, every teacher teaches his own nature to his students.

1135. Think of everything you know, then realize it has nothing in common with this higher wisdom.

1136. Placing the problem outside of ourselves is like saying that the sour fruit is independent of the tree.

1137. While words are used to explain the true path, allow your perception to travel beyond mere words.

1138. One small part of a person does not feel attacked by truth, so let offered truth fall on that right part.

1139. When seeing a clock with the wrong time we want to correct it, which is similar to the inner urge.

1140. Remember, destructive falsehood is an expert in disguising itself as constructive truth.

Look Deeper Into Facts

1141. Always try to see more in a fact you think you already understand.

1142. Being a danger to oneself simply consists of taking harmful ideas as helpful.

1143. When feeling the need for something, a right request is, "May I please have more light?"

1144. Do not fear to see your mechanical behavior, for you are opening the door to conscious action.

1145. What you will finally find will be something totally unlike anything known before.

1146. Self-awareness supplies a whole view of life, while self-centeredness is a wall which blocks the view.

1147. When really seeing self-centeredness as self-centeredness, its blocking wall begins to crumble.

1148. We contact truth at the risk of losing our familiar and beloved tears.

1149. Falsehood's first task is to betray you, and its second task is to make you think it is helping you.

1150. We can do good for ourselves only when knowing the nature of goodness, and it does not include self-strain.

1151. The dull ache felt while performing exciting activities is a voice urging you to break out of false happiness.

1152. If you would sacrifice a rock for a ruby then sacrifice what you now have for what you can have.

1153. Be aware of how your own attitudes and actions attract uncomfortable situations, for that will help end them.

1154. Abandon anything that tries to take your mind away from your great task of self-union.

1155. Be aware that you do not want to do what you know you must do, for that will help you do it.

1156. One way to think in a new and healthy way is to dare to start doing it.

1157. "Look within" is both the most helpful and most frightening advice a beginner can hear.

1158. Truth asks us to end our false ideas about existence so that it can give us the true existence we really desire.

1159. Learn the secret of using unhappy events to realize your actual freedom from unhappy events.

1160. See the difference between a harmful emotion, such as envy, and a healthy feeling, such as a yearning for self-wholeness.

Your Right Daily Start

1161. Start the day by reminding yourself, "My aim today is to shake off my unconscious psychic sleep."

1162. Be grateful that the rightness of an awakened man will not accept the wrongness of a sleeping man.

1163. The deeper you descend within yourself the higher you ascend within yourself.

1164. Right rebellion is to cease to obey the deceitful dictators within ourselves.

1165. When feeling helpless there is great power in *not turning to the usual sources of aid.*

1166. Trying to convince ourselves that we are not deceived is a good way to remain deceived.

1167. The only way to be your own best friend is to stop believing you already are.

1168. We can be truly sensible and truly practical, and then we do not go wrong.

1169. Each time we decline to place another person under fear we release ourselves from fear.

1170. Using the word "love" does not make anyone loving any more than saying the word "tulip" turns you into that flower.

1171. To uplift your treatment by others uplift your treatment of yourself.

1172. We pay a heavy price for lack of self-knowledge, even though unaware of the dreadful price.

1173. We can find a thousand excuses for not facing ourselves as we really are, and each one guarantees our secret anguish.

1174. Just to see how we endlessly repeat our self-damaging behavior is a small but definite light along the path.

1175. An awakened teacher knows much more

about his students than his students realize.

1176. By performing the same right actions that other people have performed you can win the same real rewards they have won.

1177. We have learned the limits of ourselves, which means we must now unlearn them.

1178. Being tolerant of life-robbing ideas is like tolerating a gang of ruthless bandits.

1179. If life is difficult it is simply because the person has not corrected his difficult self.

1180. Awareness of weakness attracts a new force which will be strong for you.

How to Make It

1181. Always take one more inner step than you want to take and you will make it!

1182. Bravely see how you really feel about something, which may be the opposite of what you think you feel.

1183. Inner unity starts by seeing the difference between what we say and what we really feel.

1184. The less you run away from yourself the sooner you will have a self with whom to live in ease.

1185. Truth leaves the door wide open for everyone, but it does politely inform, "Please leave your junk outside."

1186. Place a wish to understand between you and what happens to you and understanding will come.

1187. Personal problems are solved by personal rightness, never by asking others for something.

1188. What would you give for a life in which you had no need to plead with anyone for anything?

1189. There is a right way to escape from destructive people, and you are now learning it.

1190. The truly valuable part of a human being is the part by which he sees through himself.

1191. We really understand a spiritual principle when it acts spontaneously in our place.

1192. Our task is not to change our life-scenery, but to lift the mental fog that distorts its charm.

1193. The practice of suspending impulsive judgment permits the entrance of higher explanations.

1194. It is not only good but absolutely necessary to begin to doubt the power of the artificial self.

1195. Your recovered rightness always knows how to handle the wrongness of other people.

1196. Rightness does not arise from the habitual mind, but from cosmic comprehension.

1197. Great secrets come to those who sacrifice concealed conceit in order to obtain them.

1198. Take one attitude that you sense is wrong for you and deliberately drop it a dozen times a day.

1199. The upward path begins with the clear conviction that there is no substitute whatever for Truth.

1200. Concentrate everything you have into the enjoyable attainment of inner success.

13

Replace the Nervous
with the Natural

A small child was afraid of the dark. So for several nights in a row his father led him by the hand into the darkness, explaining the surrounding conditions. "These are mere shadows, not monsters," the father informed. "And that sound is simply the wind passing through the trees." With understanding, the child's fear vanished.

Here is an example of how understanding replaces uncertainty: Have you ever found yourself arguing with yourself over a problem? Self-insight would show that we gain a false and wasteful thrill over the very argument. That insight makes us want to stop, after which a calm mind sees the solution to the problem.

You need never feel yourself too frail to obtain self-command. And you need never feel disqualified by past or present wrongdoing. All you need is to start now, work now, persist now. Read and feel the brilliant beauty in these words of Frenchman Francoise Fenelon: "Never let us be discouraged with ourselves. It is not when we are conscious of our faults that we are the most wicked, on the contrary, we are less so. We see by a brighter light, and let us remember for our consolation, that we never perceive our sins until we begin to cure them."

The following lessons show how your recovered powers of naturalness dismiss nervousness once and for all.

Replace the Nervous
with the Natural

1201. These teachings help you to turn the pressures of life into forces for self-healing.

1202. Help heal yourself right now by realizing that anxiety is simply a misuse of life-energy.

1203. If you do not know how to explain life you need only relax and let True Life explain itself to you.

1204. How your world will brighten if only you will release your real nature into it!

1205. An action performed with cosmic naturalness releases right and pleasant feelings.

1206. Truth says to a timid person, "Be as scared as you want when approaching me, but be sure to approach."

1207. A crisis is wasted when it falls on anxiety instead of on an attempt to use it for new insight.

1208. Ponder whether there might be higher values than the ones now causing so much tension.

1209. One higher value is to follow your own basic intelligence, free from social influence.

1210. Reveal yourself to yourself, and regardless of what you see, continue to walk forward on the path.

1211. Realize that truth is feared at first, for this insight helps to end this false fear.

1212. Seeing and dissolving self-contradictions is one of the healthiest tasks anyone can perform.

1213. You win back your natural self by seeing the difference between it and the artificial self.

1214. Tension in any situation means that the artificial self is present, not your real nature.

1215. Natural responses to life are as close as your willingness to detect and drop unnatural responses.

1216. Defense of weakness increases it, but an effort to see unawareness as its cause decreases it.

1217. Never argue with wrongness in yourself or others, but simply walk away in perfect freedom.

1218. Inform yourself that anxiety is a hoax committed by mental imps who can be exposed and dismissed.

1219. Ordinary life puts pressure on you, so why not seek the extraordinary life having no pressure?

1220. A chief feature of the human jungle is tense unnaturalness which is called natural.

Confusion Has No Power

1221. Confusion has no real power, so continue to study these lessons in spite of all confusions.

1222. Most people react wrongly to rescue, "But if you take away my suffering, who will I be?"

1223. One day you will have the relief of not needing to anxiously ask who you are.

1224. Surface personality always pretends it is not surface personality, which is why it is always so nervous.

1225. See someone trying to act right without being right and you see a nervous wreck.

1226. The natural is obtained after a clear recognition of the unnatural causes us to drop it.

1227. Remember that even a brief glimpse into self-deception allows a ray of real light to reach you.

1228. Trembling through life is unnecessary because its cause, which is unawareness, is unnecessary.

1229. One way to remain anxious is to pretend to understand human nature.

1230. Some people find false pleasure in being upset, but a sincere seeker will have nothing to do with this.

1231. When you are not who you used to be you will not suffer from what you used to suffer.

1232. The mind obeys rightly when obeying its present natural freedom instead of submitting to past influences.

1233. Be bold in departing from the familiar but dark, for that leads to the new and the light.

1234. A willingness to be wrong is not the same as saying or imagining we are willing to be wrong.

1235. The sure cure for every anxiety is to permit cosmic truth to be your only authority.

1236. Real understanding, life-lifting understanding, never contains negative feelings of any kind.

1237. Society is unnatural, so we attain the truly natural by not imitating society.

1238. Nervousness is a state suffered by those who do not know, but who pretend that they do know.

1239. Truth does not see you as a helpless victim of life, so why see yourself that way?

1240. Trying to claim life as a personal possession and trying to grab a handful of air are equally futile.

How to End Distress

1241. Let your cosmic nature understand a distressing condition and it will cease to be a distress.

1242. Do not believe in emotions which try to make you feel alone and abandoned.

1243. Only your real nature knows when to be serious and when to be light-hearted, so let it instruct you.

1244. The more you struggle rightly with these ideas the less you struggle wrongly with life.

1245. Does it make sense to continue to trust the usual ways of thinking which have betrayed us so long?

1246. Fear fades by seeing that fear of the world is actually fear of the artificial self.

1247. Only the cosmic view can end the heartache and confusion of the human view.

1248. Bitterness is a burden which is lifted by the constant application of these higher facts.

1249. It is delightful to see that the rules you

are asked to follow are the pleasant rules of your own free nature.

1250. Stop trying to force a solution and you will happily feel the arrival of the Solution.

1251. We fall down for no other reason than our habit of leaning on nothing which we call something.

1252. There is such a thing as natural understanding, which appears spontaneously when artificiality fades.

1253. We suffer to the exact degree that we wish to hear lies instead of facts.

1254. See the difference between submitting to a belief and submitting to pure truth–and you will be different.

1255. Nervousness is a result of wrongly believing that we have a separate self to protect.

1256. Aim for that wonderful inner state which has no need to be on tense guard against anything.

1257. Be real, for then you are not the victim of the artificiality of other people.

1258. One reward of mental clearness is the absence of a strained attempt to prove that others are wrong.

1259. As a valuable test, notice that a right action will not include agitated and frightened feelings, while a wrong action will always contain these self-harming states.

1260. The fear that other people may see through us is conquered by courageously seeing through ourselves.

Your Doubts Will End

1261. The unnatural self always doubts itself, so when it fades through self-insight, doubt also fades.

1262. Everyone burdened with mechanical religion wishes he could toss it off and live naturally.

1263. Let your mind be an alert sentry at the gate which prevents enemy ideas from slipping inside.

1264. A free human being cannot be insulted because it never occurs to him that he is.

1265. The sure way to conquer confusions along the path is to continue to walk forward while surrounded by them.

1266. Each time you feel overwhelmed by life

you should remind yourself that the feeling is *unnecessary.*

1267. The real person is one who does not do damage while calling it love or generosity or community cooperation.

1268. Cosmic naturalness keeps you in calm command when everyone else dashes around in dangerous panic.

1269. We are happily right only when having no strained need to prove it to ourselves or others.

1270. These teachings cause artificial cheerfulness to give way to natural and effortless good cheer.

1271. Study anxiety and you will find it includes the pointless protection of false ideas.

1272. Whatever you do, do it consciously, then notice how much better you do!

1273. Conceal nervousness and we become its victim, but study nervousness and we become its conqueror.

1274. Letting go of your conditioned self is the same as letting go of your troubles.

1275. Our daily collisions are made up of insistences that fantasies be facts.

1276. Absorbed truth is wherever you are, so

why be nervous wherever you are?

1277. When living rightly we no longer feel like a keg of dynamite which an outside spark can explode.

1278. Nothing is more useless than to worry and wonder what other people think about you.

1279. Instead of thinking of what others think about you, think of the relief of not needing to think such thoughts.

1280. Honest inner action causes tension and nervousness to lose its hold on us.

Be Natural and Be Restful

1281. Your real nature is very restful because it never needs to promote or protect itself.

1282. Justifying anger does not reduce by one ounce the weight the anger has placed upon the justifier.

1283. Nervousness is conquered by making it conscious, and a first step in that is to set aside a pretense of calmness.

1284. Internal conflict disappears as we cease to obtain a false pleasure from it.

1285. Feeling helpless is the result of trying to

make the invented personality do the work of true being.

1286. You possess physical objects rightly when you win or lose them with the same inner poise.

1287. Your real nature never struggles for an answer, for its very nature is the whole answer, just as an eagle naturally understands the nature of an eagle.

1288. These teachings purify the emotions, making them natural powers for life-command.

1289. The man who believes he is anxious over something will one day see with great astonishment that he was anxious over nothing.

1290. Nervousness fades away by itself as we cease to insist that our trash is a treasure.

1291. What is real in you will make itself known to the exact degree that you invite it.

1292. The beauty of natural living appears as we gladly abandon the unconscious roles we are playing.

1293. Nothing condemns you but your own mistaken beliefs, and they can be replaced with truth.

1294. Develop the small part of you that knows very well the folly of following shaky society.

1295. The only world with which a man is really at war is the world within his own psychic system.

1296. Restlessness has a cure which is found only in the temple of cosmic knowledge.

1297. Having heard that you must break out of yourself, spend your days in understanding and doing it.

1298. Association with an awakened man provides both a map for the journey and courage for traveling.

1299. Dropping unnatural behavior is at first a shock and then a revelation and then a prize.

1300. Your real nature is strengthened and refreshed each time you try to understand a spiritual lesson.

14

Give New Meaning and Purpose to Life

Seeking a sunken treasure ship, a diver swam through dark waters off the coast of an island in the West Indies. For awhile he saw only the familiar scenes of rocks and sand. But suddenly he glimpsed an unfamiliar shape, something not part of the usual scene. It proved to be the faint outlines of the treasure ship.

Inner treasure consists of something not yet familiar, of something totally new to the mind. A new mind creates a new life.

The treasure which gives real meaning and purpose to our days can be found because it exists. It exists within everyone. But we need a method for its recovery. The next paragraph explains a classic method taught over the centuries by the great teachers and wise men.

Slow down. That is the secret method for mental clearness. Deliberately slow down the pace of your thoughts, feelings, words, reactions and other activities. At first you will feel a protesting shock, for the swift momentum of your usual way does not want to cooperate. Your very awareness of this resistance is a good lesson in itself. Just ignore the protests of your habitual nature and continue to slow down. If catching yourself speeding up, slow down again. It is like tugging back on the reins on rushing horses.

As you proceed with this chapter, slow down your reading and thinking a bit. Notice the curious feeling it awakens. That feeling is the door to a life rich with new meaning.

Give New Meaning and Purpose to Life

1301. The purpose of life is to lose delusions about ourselves and to find God, Truth, Reality.

1302. The moment we stop calling a meaningless life meaningful we begin to find the meaningful.

1303. Ponder and review the inspiring fact that life can be seen with a totally fresh viewpoint.

1304. The urge for a new life is right, but remember that this newness must be mental, inward, spiritual, simple.

1305. These teachings are the astounding answers to anyone who is tired of being who he now is.

1306. The treasure map consists of right thoughts and honest feelings which finally lead to the treasure itself.

1307. Awareness of how we fear the truth aids in rejecting the fear and accepting the truth.

1308. You can choose what is truly good for you, and even a small right choice has great power.

1309. We are teachable when permitting the

present way to reveal the urgent need for the new way.

1310. One small attempt to understand the inner world will do more for us than a thousand books or lectures.

1311. Darkness and wrongness are simply unconscious states which vanish in the light of consciousness.

1312. A real seeker is one who senses that the world can only pretend to fill his emptiness.

1313. Awareness of the emptiness of our lives awakens energy for finding new meaning in Reality.

1314. You have something much better to do with your life than to yield it to secret despair.

1315. The much better thing you have to do is to let cosmic light banish the darkness.

1316. Feeling emotional pain simply means you believe that the pain is *you*, which it is not.

1317. See emotional pain as a foreign invader which tries to deceive you into thinking it has power over you.

1318. Listen carefully to these facts and one day you will suddenly hear and understand something for the first time that you believed you had always understood.

1319. Truth wants to break through, tries to break through, needing only our affectionate welcome.

1320. Inner tasks which make dim sense at the start finally become the only sensible tasks we have.

True Love

1321. When doing something your essence says is right, you are in love in the right way.

1322. Mechanical action returns a false reward, while the reward of conscious action is real.

1323. Practice at listening to your inner self, and after hearing many errors you will finally hear rightness.

1324. Sense that inner light alone can supply a life-meaning which does not change every day.

1325. The journey goes forward with ease simply by traveling on while never asking, "How far is it?"

1326. Suffering starts to fade the moment we become aware of our peculiar fondness for it.

1327. Recall unhappy events in your life, then remember that a new self will prevent their repetition.

1328. If you would rather be yourself you are doing nicely by reading these pages.

1329. The persistent collection of self-knowledge is part of true spiritual work.

1330. It is a wonderful feeling to begin to see that you need not react to life in the usual doubtful ways.

1331. Let these principles make you think–think, for example, that a totally New Way exists.

1332. When puzzled just remember that all answers reside on the inner mountain peak.

1333. The part of you that wants to escape the jungle *is not confused,* indeed, it is a preliminary power for clarity.

1334. A strong feeling that you are going nowhere in life can start you going somewhere.

1335. The very fact that you do not want to continue with your present ways is a valuable message to be heeded.

1336. A first step is to know the truth mentally, while a second step is to be the truth cosmically.

1337. The desire to appear right must yield to the yearning to be right.

1338. To value true spiritual lessons and to value your life rightly are the same thing.

1339. These teachings are necessary simply because millions of people cry more than they show.

1340. Give in to the urge to discover and dissolve an inner source of anxiety.

Exploration Reveals Meaning

1341. We fear to explore the meaning of life for fear there may not be one, but exploration alone reveals real meaning.

1342. Turn your vision toward the other land, for that will arouse your urge to travel toward it.

1343. We are kept ill by society's definition of quality, for only cosmic quality can cure us.

1344. Whatever needs to fall away from your life will do so of itself as self-knowledge advances.

1345. If you want to follow powerful advice, follow, "Make yourself known to yourself."

1346. Yearn to be your own judge between right and wrong and the inner instructor will teach you.

1347. Wrongness is defined as anything out of harmony with your authentic nature.

1348. Rightness is defined as anything which is in tune with who you really are.

1349. Make it your supreme aim to remove everything that blocks remembrance of your true self.

1350. Try to see, for in the higher world *seeing* is the same as *possessing*.

1351. You will advance faster by always giving yourself a bit more inner work than you want to do.

1352. In moments of earnestness a few people ask, "Honestly, now, what real rewards does society have for me?"

1353. Tell yourself that real escape is toward Celestial Light, and never toward anything else.

1354. You will know who you are when your memory no longer describes you.

1355. When learning how to really live we no longer wonder about the purpose of life.

1356. It is better to know sooner instead of later, so why delay the esoteric expedition?

1357. The secret door opens as we learn to listen to something other than our habitual and mechanical nature.

1358. Each time we lower our impulse to impress other people we raise our capacity for real happiness.

1359. A person with a right aim is one who aims to deliver himself from himself.

1360. The reason you should win this new way is because it will make you happier than the old way.

Your Successful Day

1361. Every day that you attempt to see things as they are in truth is a supremely successful day.

1362. By knowing the kind of person you actually are you also know why your life happens as it does.

1363. By seeing the unimportance of what we call important we see the importance of what we call unimportant.

1364. What is truly important is to relax a frantic mind to permit the entrance of celestial guidance.

1365. See the difference between mechanical thinking and consciousness and you are a new person.

1366. Earnestly yearn to become a different kind of person, for then everything can be done for you.

1367. Cease to pretend that the nightmare is a beautiful dream and life takes on a new meaning.

1368. Parts of us fight against inner awakening, which means we must detect and reject them.

1369. Knowledge of the invisible mental world is essential, for it shapes the physical world.

1370. The vague emptiness felt by a person can be followed all the way to abundance.

1371. You can either build your own world or you can accept the one handed you by society, so which do you really want?

1372. Reliance upon the truth within begins by no longer relying on the words of other people.

1373. When captured by annoying thoughts, just realize you have much higher things for your attention.

1374. The orchard is there, ready for the harvest, but an orchardist is needed.

1375. People fear that truth wants to deny them thrills, when in fact truth wishes to supply a new and unique feeling having no reaction of emptiness.

1376. Most busy activities are frantic evasions of the real business of facing and finding oneself.

1377. Fear mounts up to become terror–just before you give up and break through to the new land.

1378. A real hero is someone who is trying to learn what it means to live rightly.

1379. Anyone who really wants to change inner conditions needs only to study and practice these esoteric teachings.

1380. It is good to see your inability to handle a crisis, for now you can go beyond yourself to cosmic competence.

Obtain Cosmic Gems

1381. Fill the inner emptiness with cosmic gems, not with society's follies, for gems alone can fill the emptiness.

1382. Dare to depart from self-concern in even a small way and you will feel the warmth of cosmic sunshine.

1383. The evidence of the rightness of these teachings will be seen in your own transformed nature.

1384. This training helps you to not be careless and wasteful with your life.

1385. Instead of being aggressive toward a difficulty, be quiet before it, and notice the new feeling.

1386. A new life exists and it exists for you, so what will you do with that wonderful fact?

1387. Anyone who does not like living with himself should realize the existence of a new and enjoyable self.

1388. The problem of living with our negative nature is solved by inviting our celestial nature.

1389. Cosmic principles are the wings with which we fly to a totally new kind of life-success.

1390. Learn to see what you cannot now see, and you will live what you cannot now live.

1391. Speed the day when your great passion in life is to shake yourself awake.

1392. Let everything that happens to you today contribute to your great goal of inner illumination.

1393. The one way to understand the earthly is to first understand the heavenly.

1394. By returning to where we should be we effortlessly have what we should have.

1395. Say with feeling, "I want to *know*" and you will be heard instantly and answered helpfully.

1396. The real is the essential, for the real part of a man does not want to hurt himself or others.

1397. Life can be loved only when truly understood, so now you have the perfect reason for attaining understanding.

1398. To exchange bubbles for pearls we must first be aware that bubbles are bubbles.

1399. Hear these facts with the depths of your being, not merely with the surface mind.

1400. Let go and let yourself be drawn toward the cosmic castle that is not part of this world.

15

Your Healthy Life Outside the Jungle

An ambitious king pleaded with his geographers to discover a new land for conquest. The famous geographers failed, but an obscure scholar succeeded. The scholar told the monarch about the inner kingdom. Astonished and pleased, the king turned toward self-conquest.

Genuine and permanent satisfaction comes as we turn toward and discover the inner kingdom.

Like that enlightened monarch, we must

wish to venture beyond the visible world we may now take as the only world. The very wish is energy expended in the right direction. Once catching our first glimpse of a greater world, we no longer wish to remain within the old boundaries. We are urged onward by something higher than ourselves. This is an inspiring urge we should follow gladly.

The world of self-newness is what you really want. You can sense why this is so. It is the answer to all questions and the solution to all difficulties. So seek it now. Let nothing, absolutely nothing, stand in the way of your attainment. Remember, whatever may now look like an insurmountable obstacle will one day be seen as nothing. Prove all this to yourself. It is possible. It can be done. You can do it.

When finishing this chapter, return to the start of the book. Read it again. Be happily receptive. Notice how thoughts about these principles are now joined by pleasant emotions. Now you are feeling the truth that makes you free. Let the feelings flow freely. Now you are on the way at last.

Your Healthy Life
Outside the Jungle

1401. What a curious and pleasant and healthy experience to be charmed by Truth.

1402. Your opportunity to win self-newness is right now, so go after it right now.

1403. Firmness with yourself will be rewarded with the feeling that you have done something healthy.

1404. A wise seeker firmly informs his own fantasies that he will no longer tolerate them.

1405. If only you could see that a disastrous choice in the past has no hold on you today!

1406. You can prevent one error from creating a second error by seeing the real cause of the first error.

1407. Acceptance by God, Truth, Reality simply means to see the absence of separation in the first place.

1408. Everything is all right with Truth, and always will be right.

1409. Join yourself with Truth, and everything is all right and always will be right.

1410. The comprehension that starts with a

faint glow will one day become a bright blaze of guiding light.

1411. Depression is nothing more than a cunning hoax played upon a sleeping mind, which awakening can expose.

1412. If depressed, read several ideas in this book, for that weakens the false power of depression.

1413. The burdens imposed by ordinary life are lifted the moment we want nothing more to do with ordinary life.

1414. Action and speech arising from inner trueness will always be calm, clear, right, attractive.

1415. The truly good cannot be lost, so since only the harmful can be lost, lose it today.

1416. To learn from an experience means to take it consciously, which frees us of it.

1417. The miracle of self-healing occurs when the inner patient yields to the inner physician.

1418. Circumstances are conquered simply by having no egotistical need to conquer them.

1419. When you cannot think your way out of a problem, let go and let a higher power succeed for you.

1420. Books that tell the truth become very attractive to people who really want the truth.

You Will Reach Home

1421. Keep your eyes on the light ahead, no matter how dim it may be, and you will arrive home.

1422. We are asked to go forward, not with confidence or understanding, but simply to go forward.

1423. Uplift yourself by choosing to understand something instead of fighting it.

1424. Declare, "I choose to understand" and let the energy in this right statement work for you.

1425. Self-command or self-chaos is the simple test of whether or not we are living with our true self.

1426. The physical view is sometimes beautiful, but the cosmic view is always majestic.

1427. Can anyone really straighten out his life without first straightening himself?

1428. The moment you see what it means to rise above ordinary thought–you are free.

1429. Discovering cosmic truth is like entering an immense orchard having every variety of needed and healthy fruit.

1430. One healthy shock is to see that truth will not let us get away with our usual evasions.

1431. Make fifty mistakes a day if necessary, but after each one remember your aim to escape the jungle.

1432. The true way of knowing yourself includes neither self-praise nor self-blame, but only a wise silence.

1433. Anyone who is not a problem to himself does not find other people to be a problem to him.

1434. What a man calls *his world* does not exist, but happily, *The World* certainly exists.

1435. Just as surely as distress must follow self-deceit, healing must follow self-honesty.

1436. If you wish a new and lasting good feeling, unify yourself, for self-unity always feels good.

1437. What surface personality sees as unfair is seen as nothing by your awakened essence.

1438. Something within that is not the usual you knows all the answers unknown by the usual you.

1439. Insight is growing when you detect the difference between human cleverness and cosmic wisdom.

1440. If you wish to overcome the exterior world you need only triumph in the interior world.

A Refreshing Atmosphere

1441. There is a healthy and refreshing atmosphere in a group of people who meet to *really* wake up.

1442. Cosmic consciousness creates a right consistency–consistent wisdom, strength, gentleness.

1443. Remember, you are not trying to repair the old psychic house, but building a totally new mansion.

1444. Your real strength does not reside on the level of ordinary thoughts, but is an expression of the Cosmic Whole.

1445. A decision made by a confused self will only make things worse, so seek self-clarity.

1446. Real happiness consists of a harmony

between all the parts of your nature, such as feelings harmonizing with words, or thoughts harmonizing with actions.

1447. There is no boredom along the cosmic path, for every step provides new excitements and refreshments.

1448. Remember that cosmic excitements and refreshments are totally different from previous experiences.

1449. A weary seeker was told by a wise man, "Replace unconscious fighting with conscious listening."

1450. Become aware of how habitual thought acts as a barrier to fresh and inspiring impressions.

1451. Each time a man excuses weakness in himself he lowers the quality of life in the entire world.

1452. Each time a man seeks inner strength he raises the quality of life in the entire world.

1453. Now that you have facts about self-awakening, go on to the experience.

1454. You can carry this quiet and secret world with you right in the midst of the noisy world.

1455. Your aim is to know that these teachings

are right, not because someone else says so, but because they have changed you into a new kind of human being.

1456. Discouragement fades by seeing that higher forces within can do what lower forces cannot do.

1457. Learn to spend your thoughts as profitably as you now try to spend your money.

1458. When you react wrongly remind yourself, "I can do better than that the next time."

1459. The supremely wise reason for studying the self is to end the troubles it causes.

1460. Self-concern is banished by seeing that we have a completely different self than we imagined.

Your Good News

1461. Hear the good news that we can stop buying bad dreams and invest our lives in real wealth.

1462. The only escape we need is to escape from delusions about ourselves.

1463. As a summary you can say that your cosmic aim is to remember who you really are.

1464. Let "Self-change through self-knowledge" be one of your favorite quotations.

1465. A whole mind can switch from the heavenly to the earthly and back again with quiet ease.

1466. One day you will truly go your own way, knowing from yourself that the world has nothing for you.

1467. Whoever admits even one small confusion in himself has given the world a gift greater than a thousand rubies.

1468. The supreme daring which changes everything is to dare to step outside of yourself.

1469. Step outside of yourself right now by not assuming that your life must remain as it is.

1470. Nothing real prevents your return to your cosmic homeland, so let nothing prevent it.

1471. Collecting right ideas is great, but remembering to act from them is tremendous.

1472. Save yourself from yourself, then see whether you need to be saved by or from anyone else.

1473. Become your own healthy atmosphere, for then a noisy office is your own quiet home.

1474. It is the retreat into the familiar that prevents an advance into the healing.

1475. Real happiness depends upon the amount of the usual self we *do not live from.*

1476. Rescuing truth announces its presence, then waits to see what people will do with it.

1477. The firmness of an authentic teacher is a lofty kind of compassion.

1478. A wise student says, "Now that I have heard that fact I will climb until understanding it."

1479. Never fear to deliberately walk through dark places, for that is how you reach the light on the other side.

1480. One by one the lights go on until we see astonishing sights we never before knew existed.

Use These Cheery Reminders

1481. You have simply forgotten your true identity, but these facts are cheerful reminders.

1482. To see the truly new beyond the self we must not fearfully cling to the self.

1483. See that you are not your ideas about yourself and you will finally see who you really are.

1484. It is not fearful to be a nobody, for fear arises only when falsely believing we must be important.

1485. If conditions were new, you would not be new, but if you were new, conditions would be new.

1486. There is a Power which can think and live for us far better than we can think and live for ourselves.

1487. The real part of you can reject a negative atmosphere just as easily as a stone wall rejects a breeze.

1488. If you want to know what to do, just do what is right and ignore the consequences.

1489. Every fact of this cosmic science is far more important than appears on the surface, so dig deeply for richer rewards.

1490. With your consent these ideas will give you different and higher feelings toward yourself.

1491. One day you will look back to the kind of world you used to live in and be very glad you no longer do.

1492. When finally realizing that confusion

cannot understand confusion, the mind rises to clear comprehension.

1493. When conditions are wrong but you are right, everything is all right.

1494. Seeing the necessity for self-insight, not assuming we already have it, is a sign of real intelligence.

1495. Rise above mere knowledge to a higher level of being, for that is where self-command exists.

1496. Remember the feeling of rightness in these ideas, for remembrance is power for progress.

1497. Know that you are not seeking comfort, but understanding, and in understanding there is true comfort.

1498. Call anything good which enables you to see more today than you saw yesterday.

1499. Permit these ideas to change you internally and watch how you delightfully value them more and more.

1500. The lamp has been placed before you, so take it as your own guiding light from this day on.

209

Notes

Notes

Notes

Notes

Notes